PERSONAL, SOCIAL AND MORAL EDUCATION

To Hazel, Martyn and Graham

See, a king will reign in righteousness
     and rulers will rule with justice.
Each man will be like a shelter from the wind
     and a refuge from the storm,
like streams of water in the desert
     and the shadow of a great rock in a thirsty land.

The prophet Isaiah

PERSONAL, SOCIAL AND MORAL EDUCATION

A SOURCE BOOK

BRIAN WAKEMAN

A LION BOOK

Tring · Belleville · Sydney

Copyright © 1984 Lion Publishing

Published by
Lion Publishing plc
Icknield Way, Tring, Herts, England
ISBN 0 85648 650 7
Albatross Books
PO Box 320, Sutherland, NSW 2232, Australia
ISBN 0 86760 563 4

First edition 1984

Acknowledgements
All the photographs in this book are the author's

Graphics by Tony Cantale

Bible quotations are from the *New International Version,* copyright
1978 by New York International Bible Society

Other copyright material reprinted from the following: 'Full List of
Moral Components' in *The Ethical Dimension of the School Curriculum,*
edited by L. O. Ward, University College of Swansea; *Lifeline,* P.
McPhail, H. Chapman, T. R. Ungoed-Thomas, 1972, Schools Council
Moral Education Project, Longman Group Ltd; *Meeting Yourself
Halfway,* S. Simon, 1974, Argus Communications; 'Moral Stages and
Moralization', Lawrence Kohlberg in *Moral Development and Behavior,*
edited by Thomas Lickona, copyright © 1976, Holt, Rinehart and
Winston, reprinted by permission of Holt, Rinehart and Winston, CBS
College Publishing; *Promoting Moral Growth,* R. Hersh, D. P. Paolitto
and J. Reimer, Longman Inc; *Values and Teaching,* Raths et al, 1978,
Charles E. Merrill Publishing Company

Printed in Spain by ELEXPURU, S. A. L.—Bilbao

Contents

Introduction

This book arose from an article in *The Sunday Times* and subsequent programmes for the British Broadcasting Corporation. There are already many publications on the theory and practice of Personal, Social and Moral Education and a wide choice of excellent teaching materials. I have learnt much from them. But very few are written by practising teachers. This, then, is the first justification for writing this book. I am a teacher writing about my own craft. Many teachers have been kind enough to comment that they have found my contribution to in-service courses and conferences on pastoral care or social education of help and inspiration. I offer this book to other teachers, passing on what I have learnt as a teacher for their critical appraisal.

My second reason for assembling the material in this book is quite different. Most books on Personal, Social and Moral Education are written from an ideological perspective which I find only partially satisfying, or which gives me cause for concern because of the implicit value assumptions built into the teaching method, materials or the aims of the unit of work. I would be the first to applaud the work, ideas and insights, and in some cases the practical class-room materials, other authors have provided. I could not work without them, and I quote extensively from them in this book. What I have not seen is very much work written from a Christian view of life, and particularly one which relates Christian beliefs to teaching practice. There are many articles, books, talks and opinions expressed from the broadly 'Humanist' view of life, or from a 'Marxist' perspective on education, but too few from the standpoint of a Christian faith.

My second reason for writing this book therefore springs from my own Christian faith. I believe, to use New Testament language, that the 'lordship of Christ' applies as much to our working life as it does to our family or to the church community. I want God's rule to influence my practice as a teacher of Personal, Social and Moral Education. I realize that this is a controversial statement, but it is my desire, in St Paul's words, to 'take captive every thought to make it obedient to Christ'.

There are two leading assertions in this book:
- Personal, Social and Moral Education should feature high in our principles for the selection of the curriculum, and be clearly evident in our translation of aims into the real education of our pupils.
- Christians have a distinctive contribution to make both to the debate about the theory of Personal, Social and Moral Education, and to its practice in our schools.

I have arranged the material in three sections which I invite my fellow-teachers and other interested people to consider and evaluate in the light of their own situation and experience.

Part 1 contains a survey of the upsurge of interest in this area in Britain as I have perceived it. There is an attempt to clarify what is meant by Personal, Social and Moral Education, and I argue the case why all teachers, and schools as a whole, should concern themselves with this area of education. There are philosophical assumptions underlying all teaching and learning, particularly in this area. I have attempted to identify possible value assumptions in some approaches and to offer a critique of them, or point out my own reservations. Finally, I argue the case for the distinctive contribution that Christians can make to this dimension of the curriculum.

If Part 1 was the backcloth, **Part 2** is the dialogue, or at least one side of it. The other part is the reader's own response to my writing. Part 2 begins with a chapter on planning principles, discussing aims and their influence on teaching method. The question is raised of whether distinctive Christian aims are justifiable in a state school, and the importance of a match between the aims of the school and of PSME. Issues of organization and approach to timetabling PSME are then dealt with. A number of hypotheses are raised which I believe will lead to an effective programme. The questions of content and teaching method, and the selection of materials are raised as problematic. Some suggestions for content are offered, examples of materials are given and a critique is put forward. I have offered some principles which I have found

lead to more successful work in the class-room. This area of content, appropriate pedagogy, and selection of class-room learning materials must be left ultimately to those responsible in the local community, together with the teachers, to work out. The needs of a rural community in Africa might be totally different from communities in Singapore or Australia. The critical incidents in school life, the problems of identity, the preparation for adult life in one society, are likely to be very different from another. Finally in this section I suggest some ways I have found of trying to evaluate Personal, Social and Moral Education.

If Part 1 is the backcloth and Part 2 the dialogue, **Part 3** might be called the props, or the extended bibliography. This is in no way exhaustive, but refers to writers on theory and practice, class-room materials, projects and other class-room aids which I have found particularly helpful.

The readers are invited to respond to the arguments, weigh the principles suggested in the light of their own experience and situation, and test the hypotheses. Above all, they are encouraged to reflect about the way the needs of the young people in their care are being met, as they grow up into young adults. It is my hope that this book will create discussion, debate and—more importantly— action, to contribute to the personal, social and moral development of our pupils.

PART 1

SURVEYING THE SCENE

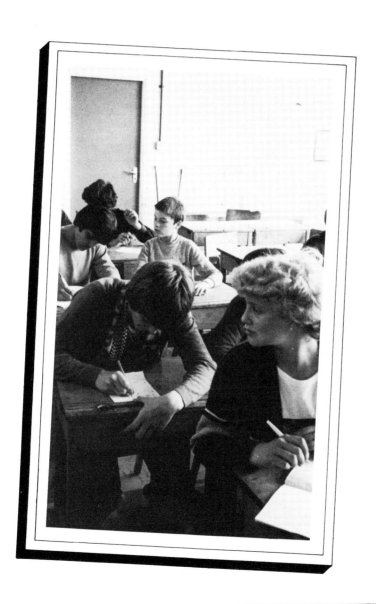

CHAPTER 1

HISTORICAL PERSPECTIVE

It seems that educators have been concerned about the personal, social and moral development of their charges since before the time of Moses. Enquiry about the nature of the 'good life', training in principles for life, the development of specific character traits, study of the writings of great minds on the nature of society, the ideals for good personal relationships . . . these have all been part of the educational diet of boys and girls down through the centuries.

There is certainly nothing new in a teacher's interest in the personal, moral or social development of the pupil.

'Hear, O Israel: The Lord our God, the Lord is one. Love the Lord your God with all your heart and with all your soul and with all your strength. These commandments that I give you today are to be upon your hearts. Impress them on your children. Talk about them when you sit at home and when you walk along the road, when you lie down and when you get up.'
Deuteronomy 6:4–7

'My son, do not forget my teaching, but keep my commands in your heart, for they will prolong your life many years and bring you prosperity.
Let love and faithfulness never leave you;
bind them around your neck, write them on the tablet of your heart.
Then you will win favour and a good name in the sight of God and man.'
Proverbs 3:1–4

'If your two sons were only colts or bullocks, we could have hired a trainer for them to make them beautiful and good and all they should be; and our trainer would have been, I take it, a horseman or a farmer. But now that they are human beings, have you any trainer in your mind for them? Is there anyone who understands what a man and citizen ought to be?'
Plato's *Apology*, Socrates speaking to Callias

'The medieval student, before the development of the college system had done its work, was riotous, lawless, and licentious . . . There can be little doubt that the habits contracted at Oxford and Cambridge account for the scandalous character of so many of the clergy in later life. The authorities of the Universities forbade athletic exercises among the youth . . . but made no great effort to keep them out of the tavern and . . . some of them roamed about in robber bands. But England found a remedy for these evils. The College system . . . parents and practical men saw the advantage of academic homes to shelter the young from the material and moral dangers possibly as bad as the intellectual errors of Wyclif.'
G. M. Trevelyan, *Illustrated English Social History*

'At some time between the ages of 14 and 18 they might go on to Oxford or Cambridge, while others completed their education as 'henchmen' or squires at the King's Court, or in court-like households of great noblemen. There the acquirements most valued were not Latin, but skill in riding, jousting at tournaments, field sports, dancing, harping, piping, and singing and doubtless all the forms of love-making. Moralists denounced these establishments as the ruin of the youth trained in them. No doubt some were better than others . . . at the latter end of the fifteenth century.'
G. M. Trevelyan

M. G. Jones, writing of the charity schools in Wales during the eighteenth century, says:
'It would be difficult to exaggerate the importance and effect of the charity school movement upon the history and character of the Welsh people. The steady concentration upon piety as the aim and end of all instruction changed a gay and simple people, indifferent in religion and lacking political consciousness, into a people whose dominate interests were religious and political.'
M. G. Jones, *The Charity School Movement, A Study of Eighteenth Century Puritanism in Action*

The quotations from different historical periods in the Judaeo-Christian tradition and social history illustrate concern about this aspect of children's development. I could equally well have chosen quotations from ancient civilizations, or Islamic sources. There appears to be a large measure of agreement among educators universally that education should include teaching about personal, moral and social development. (There is, however, considerable *dis*agreement about what should be taught, and how best to teach it. I shall return to these controversial issues in later chapters.)

Over the past fifteen years there has been a revival of interest in this area. It would have been an attractive proposition to have taken a term off, or to have applied for a school master fellowship, and have written in a university library with the advice of academics from the fields of theology, history and the disciplines of education. Instead it has been written from my own experience, in what spare time I could snatch in the busy schedule of a deputy head.

In the 1960s, teachers were strongly influenced by child-centred theories of education in their initial training. Child development was the queen of disciplines, and Piaget seemed to be the court's high priest. Words such as 'experiential' and 'relevant' had magic properties. We left our towers of learning eager to orm the battlements of the schools ith our new theories. No one had arned us about the 'dragons'— onservative headmasters, traditional abject-boundaries, and the exam-ound school curriculum. Youthful dealism took many knocks as we ettled into our new jobs. I suspect, owever, that this interest in the aild at the centre of the educational rocess is a significant contribution o later developments in Personal, ocial and Moral Education in chools. This is certainly true in my wn thinking.

Another important contribution to ne Personal, Social and Moral ducation movement was the urriculum development going on in ne world of Religious Education as t was then called in Britain. The Agreed Syllabus was coming under re from two flanks. The teachers vere finding that the Agreed yllabus (Abraham-to-the-exile and he Life of Jesus, Acts and Church History, with a few missionaries hrown in if the pupils were lucky) vas not enthusing pupils, even when aught at its best. At its worst it led o disruptive behaviour—and despair n teachers. Those who criticized the Agreed Syllabus at that time had not leard of the imaginative teaching hat was going on, sensitive to the neeeds and interests of children, and which helped them develop religious deas and values of their own.

The other guns were fired from academic circles. Names such as Harold Loukes, Ronald Goldman and later Ninian Smart come to mind as the generals of these forces.

● Loukes represented the view that religion was about life: the 'implicit' approach.

● Goldman argued that children's religious thinking developed through given stages similar to Piaget's schema. RE teaching, he held, ought o match content with these stages. The introduction of incorrect material at the wrong time, he claimed, hindered religious thinking ater on. This became known as the life themes' approach.

● Under the influence of questions about the philosophical justification for RE in a pluralistic society, Ninian Smart and his associates developed the explicit Religious Studies approach, looking at the phenomenon of religion.

This curriculum development through the Schools Council, the Christian Education Movement and County RE Advisers left some RE teachers bewildered, some stubbornly digging in their toes and continuing with Abraham-to-the-exile. Others, mostly younger teachers, joined the new RE bandwagon, and many looked to the implicit side of RE, the social/personal topics, the 'problems of young people' approach, with highlights from the Bible or other religious literature.

It is interesting how many RE-trained teachers have changed direction, moving from RE teaching into pastoral care, counselling, youth service, and curriculum development jobs. The implicit approach to RE gave birth to the beginnings of many schemes of work which would now be called Personal, Social and Moral Education.

The changes in RE teaching are better described in the Schools Council Working Paper 36, *Religious Education in Secondary Schools*. But I mention them here because of the legitimate interest RE teachers have in moral questions and the skills they have in dealing with controversial human issues. Their interest in life themes and implicit religious ideas in everyday life have led many into the Personal, Social and Moral Education world, or wider areas of the curriculum.

In the 1960s and '70s there was a spawning of curriculum development projects from the Schools Council out to teachers' centres and schools in Britain. The Schools Council, recently disbanded in its old form, was a government-funded body sponsoring and facilitating curriculum development.

Two notable Schools Council projects have had a great influence on teaching method in Personal, Social and Moral Education. The first is the Schools Council Project in Moral Education, better known as *Lifeline*, headed by Peter McPhail. The second is the Humanities Curriculum Project (HCP), developed by Lawrence Stenhouse. *Lifeline* has had a lasting impact, both through teachers still using the materials, and in setting the model for class-room materials which other projects have followed. HCP has had a deeper impression on teaching method, namely 'procedurally neutral chairmanship' when dealing with controversial issues in the class-room. I shall return to it several times in this book.

The *Lifeline* project presented me with teaching materials and methods for the class-room which I have used ever since. I began to read the theory much later in *Moral Education in the Secondary School*. I recommend teachers to go back and look at both these projects for historical interest and for practical ideas and materials which can still be used.

Undoubtedly the raising of the school-leaving age produced curriculum development, panic thinking in some circles and more creative ideas through the Schools Council working papers and projects. Teachers and curriculum planners were forced to think again about what they were going to do with the extra year, possibly with bored, obstreperous youths. How were they going to make schooling relevant, interesting, of some worth in relation to the needs of these girls and boys? What bearing could this extra year have on preparing young people for the working world, adult roles as parents, employees, citizens, and so on? I remember helping to set up experimental courses in Reading to prepare for what became known as 'ROSLA children'.

The raising of the school-leaving age was certainly a challenge to subject-centred teaching, the 'imparting of knowledge' view of teaching. A lot of interest in the social, emotional, personal and sexual aspects of children's education was generated at this time, if only for the survival of teachers at the most instrumental level. Many teachers welcomed this opportunity to get away from the exam-constrained curriculum, and the chance to begin to educate children for life.

I can now see the influence of human development educators such as Dewey and C. Rogers, and the influence of the 'comprehensive ideal', on my thinking. I became very impressed with 'wholistic' educators, having almost a psycho-therapeutic view of schooling at one time. As a head of year in a comprehensive school for boys I became very interested in counselling, pastoral care and education in personal relationships. I attended counselling courses, and took part in the sensitivity training and in education in personal relationships courses at that time. There was what almost amounted to a movement in the '70s in each of the fields of counselling,[1] education in personal relationships,[2] and pastoral care[3] which later came closer together to form one of the major thrusts in personal and social development in British schools in the 1980s.[4]

'Pastoral care' is an umbrella term for a number of activities along a continuum of concepts from 'control and discipline' at one end, through 'positive forms of organization and discipline which encourage learning in the school', to 'a system of care which promotes pupil autonomy, self-awareness, and social skills' at the other end. If you were to ask three different teachers what is understood by pastoral care in their school you would probably get as many different answers. At my own school in Luton we use the accompanying diagram 'Notions of Pastoral Care' to show what we mean by pastoral care.

I was lecturing at Klagenfurt University in Austria to a conference on action research when I mentioned pastoral care in passing. After the lecture a professor of education questioned me about the notion of pastoral care and how we organize pastoral work in the school. He was particularly interested in the legal position of teachers in England as *in loco parentis*. I mention this because I had not until then realized how odd

it was that the teachers in England should not only have the role of imparter of information, developer of mind, trainer of skills, but also have a pastoral role of 'substitute parent' while children are in his or her care. I have noticed a considerable tension between what teachers call their academic work and their pastoral role, as I have participated in and tutored at conferences on the pastoral and Personal, Social and Moral Education aspects of schooling. This tension is particularly strong when more is being required from form tutors in a 'pastoral curriculum' (see Active Tutorial Work, mentioned below). However, the majority of teachers in England, if not all, are aware of their *loco parentis* obligations to their pupils. This notion of *loco parentis* and pastoral care is important to an understanding of how Personal, Social and Moral Education has developed in England. The teacher is legally required to show the care, concern and thought for his pupils that a good parent would show.

The growth in special jobs for pastoral staff received fresh impetus from the concern about the loss of identity of individual children in large comprehensive schools of 1,000–1,500 pupils. Revision in the salary structure created new posts for heads of year, or heads of house, and for the provision of a third deputy headteacher. In many comprehensive schools a deputy headteacher, together with a year head or head of house and the form tutors, has a special responsibility for the welfare, safety, organization, administration, discipline and guidance of the pupils. Counsel, advice, encouragement, interest in the person as well as academic progress, organization of trips and social events may all be

part of the form teacher's job. Some English schools have counsellors, of course, as in the USA, but many teachers are expected to contribute t the pupil's pastoral care as well as fulfilling their academic subject-teaching role.

Another allied development which deserves mention at this point is the Pastoral Curriculum. Largely through the work and writings of Douglas Hamblin (until recently at the School of Education, Swansea University), Ken David (an Adviser in Education in Personal Relationships), and the team in Lancashire who have produced the excellent series 'Active Tutorial Work', there has been an upsurge of interest in an approach to Personal, Social and Moral Education called the 'Pastoral Curriculum'. The Pastoral Curriculum is a structured, planned approach based on the form teacher. It utilizes slack time in the registration and form period of English secondary schools. It takes up major themes such as:
self-awareness
growing independence
relationships at school
growing up
coping with school
becoming a successful learner
preparing for examinations
preparing for leaving school
making decisions and so on.

I shall look at this in more detail later. It is sufficient now to say that individual teachers or a school can customize the suggestions in these books to suit their own needs. The class-room activities suggested are an excellent source of ideas for the busy teacher. Schools all over England are now experimenting with this material, adapting it, testing it and adopting the ideas.

Teachers interested in the Pastoral Curriculum would benefit particularly from refreshing their minds about the two seminal projects developed by the Schools Council in the late 1960s and '70s—*Lifeline* and HCP. Later, in chapter three, I shall return to question the value and philosophical assumptions implicit in materials and offer some critique.

Back in the 1960s and '70s a third

WHAT DOES 'PASTORAL CARE' MEAN?

System of care promoting pupil autonomy, self-awareness and social skills training

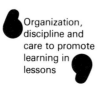
Organization, discipline and care to promote learning in lessons

Control, conformity, emphasis on the school community

NOTIONS OF PASTORAL CARE

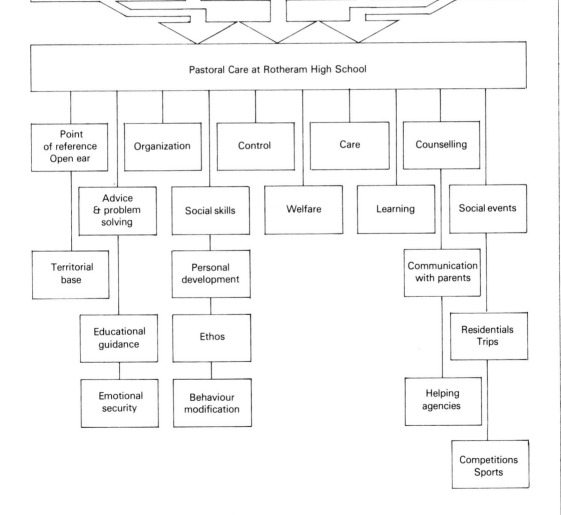

Loco parentis

e.g.
Parent provides:
- care, love, attention
- protection, food
- oversight of health and welfare
- socialization
- gradual independence

Teacher takes on some of these tasks in lieu of parent

Shepherding

e.g.
- advice, counsel, guidance
- succour in distress
- moral guide, example
- spiritual help
- individual care and concern
- ultimate good in mind
- warning, admonishing
- developing maturity
- problem solving

Pastoral care movement

e.g.
- positive discipline
- effective organization
- ethos and curriculum to develop:
  good learning
  learning skills
  pupil autonomy
  self-awareness
  social skills
- management of learning environment
- emotional development
- coping skills, choosing

Pastoral Care at Rotheram High School

| Point of reference Open ear | Organization | Control | Care | Counselling |

Advice & problem solving — Social skills — Welfare — Learning — Social events

Territorial base — Personal development — Communication with parents

Educational guidance — Ethos — Residentials Trips

Emotional security — Behaviour modification — Helping agencies

Competitions Sports

project was also making an impact on my thinking: *Community Service in the Middle Years of Schooling*. I was involved with a group of teachers at Bulmershe College near Reading who were looking at the effects of community service on pupils. I have not seen the outcome of that project, but I became convinced of the importance of community service in any programme of Personal, Social and Moral Education. We had groups of young people going out each week into the homes of senior citizens and handicapped people, ostensibly to help with shopping, gardening, mending things about the house, or to read library books. Another group went with a colleague to a hospital for mentally handicapped children. There they assisted with painting, helped in the swimming-pool and gymnasium, took youngsters for walks and played with the children.

I have no doubt that we did contribute in some measure to the community, but by far the greatest value was the experience, responsibility and practical learning of the pupils. The follow-up diaries and discussion led to real involvement and commitment to social questions and controversial human issues which other, simulated, methods of teaching rarely get.

The personal growth of individual pupils was quite striking. I remember a startling discussion about death with a group, after an old man whom we visited regularly had been taken to hospital. I also remember one lad who had been working at the children's hospital saying that he now understood his mother, who had suffered from mental illness for years. I could quote many more cases.

Community service deals with real people, living situations which are important and matter deeply to the pupils. Community service teaches the young to care about the needs of others, which is perhaps one of the greatest deficiencies of urban living.[5] The skilful teacher can help pupils to explore and understand their own feelings, prejudices and shortcomings in relation to their community service experiences.

Many social and moral education lessons lack reality. They are not pupil-centred, but detached, intellectual exercises in moral reasoning or opinion. Abstract ideas, other people's views, become the centre of the lesson. The content becomes information, and the important process for the pupil of working out 'what I think', or 'coming to terms with what I feel' can, if we are not careful, disappear. Community service has the great benefit of keeping our Personal, Social and Moral Education practical, concerned with real life, and child-centred.

The Schools Council issued a number of research studies and working papers, such as the famous *Cross'd with Adversity*, the education of socially disadvantaged children in secondary schools in 1970; or *Careers Education in the 1970s* in 1972. Another working paper which did not appear to influence people as widely at the time because of its radical proposals was WP 51, *Social Education: an experiment in four secondary schools*, published in 1974.

It so happened that the following year I moved from my job as a head of year, RE and Social Education teacher, to a new post in Luton as Co-ordinator of Social Education. This post was set up by the headmaster to develop programmes of social education throughout the school in a planned, structured and co-ordinated way.

The WP 51 became my bed-time reading for inspiration and encouragement. The radical proposals provided stimulus and challenge as I began to settle into my new post, and in time begin the innovations for which I had been employed. (I have described this elsewhere, in 'Social Education at Rotheram High School'.) I have called the WP 51 working paper radical because it encourages active pupil participation and involvement in both school and community affairs.

The ideal which animates this kind of social education harks back to the older Greek concept of democracy, where the citizens participate in running their collective affairs. The social education school should be engaged in common pursuits which

they have collectively agreed, the paper argues. I would like to encourage other teachers to go back and read these ideas, and not reject them out-of-hand. The schools in many urban societies, particularly those with high unemployment, could do well to work out the implications of the introduction to WP 51: 'One of the qualities of a good education is that it should enable young people to adapt successfully to the requirements of living in the conditions which face them now and will face them when their formal education is over.'

I am well aware that I am offering a personal view of the development of the current interest in Personal, Social and Moral Education. It can be criticized as being idiosyncratic, or as lacking historical discipline. I may have over-emphasized particular causes, omitted important factors and perhaps in places eclipsed evidence with anecdote. Serious students of the history of education can turn to other volumes!

I frequently meet teachers, advisers and academics attending conferences about this area of education who have arrived at similar interests by different routes. Some have a background in the Humanities, Moral Philosophy, or Curriculum Theory, some come from Home Economics, Biology, Sex Education, Youth Service Training, concerns about Health Education, or from Careers Education. I have not portrayed these routes because they are not dominant features on my experiential map. I have no doubt that many of these colleagues would write this chapter differently. What I have been trying to do is to introduce readers, particularly those outside the UK and those who have not experienced these happenings, to the main influences on the growth of the Personal, Social and Moral Education movement.

Careers Education has been one major influence, particularly in my own authority. Readers might like to refer to the Schools Council Project *Work* or the work of CRAC (Careers Research and Advisory Centre) to see that for many years Careers Education has not been concerned solely with information or with

matching pupils and occupations, but with familiar themes such as:
choice
preparing young people for adult roles
discussion about lifestyles, values, and opinions
helping pupils gain skills to cope in school, and later to adapt and be successful as young adults and so on.

Some Careers Departments in English secondary schools run elaborate Social Education programmes which include community service, adjustment to working life, work experience, discussion about ethical, sexual and personal problems, introduction to economic and political concepts, as well as the more usual careers information, guidance and advice. Some schools have a co-ordinated careers programme or 'guidance' as it may be called for their pupils from the ages of 13 to 18. The concerns of Careers Education about the child, his growing independence, his opinions and beliefs, equipping him with skills for his future life as an emerging adult, as well as the narrower occupational and guidance interest, has been a major thrust in the progress of Personal, Social and Moral Education.

Another thread in the DNA-like helix of Personal, Social and Moral Education is Health Education. *Living Well*, the Health Education Council's project, aims to 'promote healthy living by helping young people cope with and approach positively the challenges, complexities, difficulties and anxieties of everyday life'. The similarity to the earlier *Lifeline* project in format and content is quite striking. The Schools Council Health Education Project 5–13, *Think Well*, has as its major aim 'to help children make considered choices or decisions related to their health behaviour by increasing knowledge and clarifying beliefs and values which they hold'. These two projects have had an extensive influence on our programme of Personal, Social and Moral Education at Rotheram High School. I have found that teachers on courses have welcomed these materials for practical class-room use, so I commend them to the reader.

The change of emphasis, or rather broadening of concern, in health education from a narrower interest in medical or biological issues of hygiene in the earlier 1960s has been quite marked. When I first began to take an interest in Health Education it was with preventive notions in mind about the dangers of drugs, the effects of smoking, consequences of premarital sex (particularly the risk of venereal diseases), and the prevention of BO! At that time in Reading it was my role tactfully to counsel the children with poor hygiene.

This preventive aspect of Health

Much responsibility rests on the teacher. The busy head of year is leader and co-ordinator of a pastoral team.

Education, 'the dangers and risks', was joined by a more positive concept of health which I came across, proposed by the World Health Organization. 'Positive well-being' and the 'health triangle' (physical, mental and social) became catch-words in a broader concept of Health Education, which was to embrace a more wholistic view of health: physical, mental, social, behavioural, spiritual and emotional. I remember drawing a diagram to represent the interest in wider aspects of health.

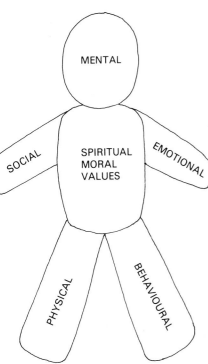

A cynical view of these new developments in RE, Careers, Social Education, Pastoral Education, Education in Personal Relationships and Health Education might be that they were political bids (by interest groups) to control a blurred, undefined area of the curriculum. There are many threads of Personal, Social and Moral Education in several different subjects and disciplines in a school curriculum. All teachers contribute to the Personal, Social and Moral Education of their pupils. Various writers and projects I have mentioned called for a unified, collaborative and co-ordinated approach to this so-called 'soft' area of the curriculum, which the Newsom Report, *Half our Future*, had invited schools to explore back in 1963. There were, no doubt, battles of power and control about traditional reserves of individual subjects when a 'whole school', 'integrated' approach to Personal, Social and Moral Education was being considered by a school. I dare to suggest that many schools still

have those particular skirmishes to face, if they respond to the central challenge of this book.

When I began to plan a Social Education course in 1975 I had a year to prepare while teaching my own subject. One of the first tasks I set about was to find out what Social Education was already taking place in the school. I examined schemes of work and talked with colleagues to establish what topics and processes were being covered, by whom and at what stage in the pupil's career. I drew up a chart to show the results of this survey, and began to design courses to fill the gaps, and extend and develop the splintered and fragmented parts.

Some years later the Schools Council Health Education Project 13–18 published a Co-ordinators' Manual which suggests ways of tackling this problem of a whole school approach to Personal, Social and Moral Education. Ken David has also written on this subject, and has much helpful advice which I could have benefited from at the time! The SCHEP Project 13–18 has rendered great service to schools by concentrating on training teachers to co-ordinate Personal, Social and Moral Education in schools. Co-ordinated approaches are still controversial in staff-rooms, but I believe SCHEP has done much to help schools solve the problems associated with a whole curriculum approach to Personal, Social and Moral Education. I believe Personal, Social and Moral Education is so important that a whole curriculum approach, carefully planned, programmed and co-ordinated is essential for all pupils.

The importance of Personal, Social and Moral Education has been underlined recently in documents circulated by the Department of Education and Science and by the Schools Council and, in a different form, by the Manpower Services Commission. The Secondary Survey Report 1975–8 concentrated on the education of pupils during their last two years of compulsory education. Personal and Social Development was one of the four aspects of the curriculum the inspectorate looked at, together with Language,

Mathematics and Science. It highlighted the importance attributed to personal and social development, not only in terms of the whole curriculum but also in trying to prepare young people for adult life. In general it concluded that the great majority of schools recognized their responsibilities in this area, but there was need for more curricular provision. Some schools had outstanding programmes but in many there was insufficient planning and co-ordination. Many schools, it said, needed to do more in preparing their pupils for living and working in the adult world.

In *A View of the Curriculum* it is stated that 'There are some sorts of knowledge—about themselves, about other people, about the nature of the world in which they are growing up—which all pupils need. Personal and Social Development in this broad sense is a major charge on the curriculum.' The analysis of the curriculum relies on check-lists of desirable experience and understanding. These are derived from philosophers of education who propose epistemological arguments for forms of knowledge, essential areas of experience or realms of meaning which the curriculum planners should use in principles of planning. The names of Paul Hirst, Philip Phenix and Michael Oakeshott, together with Richard Peters, will be familiar to both past and present students of the philosophy of education.

A check-list of aims for education is offered by *Framework for the School Curriculum* (1980). It includes:
● 'to help pupils acquire knowledge and skills relevant to adult life and employments in a fast changing world . . .
● 'to instil respect for religious and moral values, and tolerance for other races, religions, and ways of life . . .'

Later it observes that schools contribute to the preparation of young people for all aspects of adult life. 'This requires many additions to the core subjects . . . including Moral Education, Health Education, preparation for parenthood and an adult role in family life; Careers Education and vocational guidance;

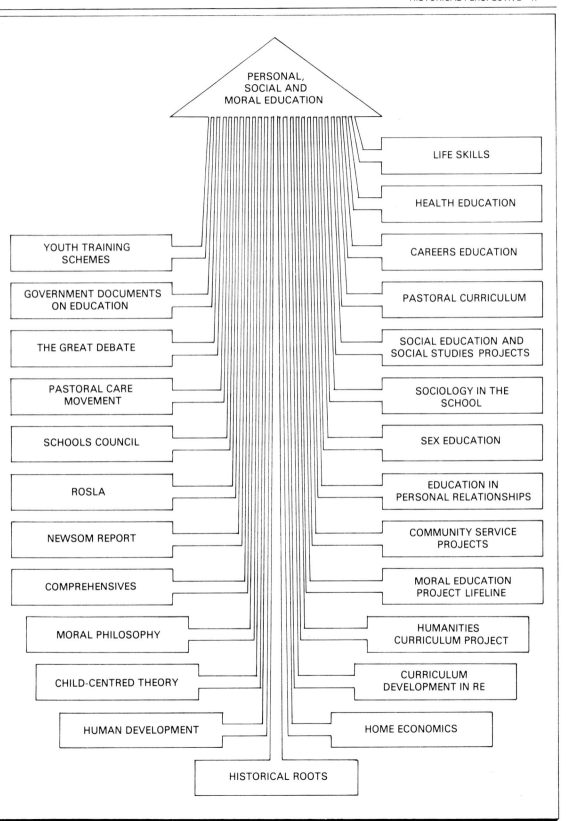

PERSONAL, SOCIAL AND MORAL EDUCATION

LIFE SKILLS

HEALTH EDUCATION

YOUTH TRAINING SCHEMES

CAREERS EDUCATION

GOVERNMENT DOCUMENTS ON EDUCATION

PASTORAL CURRICULUM

THE GREAT DEBATE

SOCIAL EDUCATION AND SOCIAL STUDIES PROJECTS

PASTORAL CARE MOVEMENT

SOCIOLOGY IN THE SCHOOL

SCHOOLS COUNCIL

SEX EDUCATION

ROSLA

EDUCATION IN PERSONAL RELATIONSHIPS

NEWSOM REPORT

COMMUNITY SERVICE PROJECTS

COMPREHENSIVES

MORAL EDUCATION PROJECT LIFELINE

MORAL PHILOSOPHY

HUMANITIES CURRICULUM PROJECT

CHILD-CENTRED THEORY

CURRICULUM DEVELOPMENT IN RE

HUMAN DEVELOPMENT

HOME ECONOMICS

HISTORICAL ROOTS

and preparation for a participatory role in adult society . . . at one stage or another . . . all should find a place in the education of every pupil.'

All these documents, and others I do not have space to mention, have been hotly debated in the educational press, and endlessly argued over in institutions of higher education. Some commentators have interpreted them as attempts by politicians to bring greater control and centralization to the curriculum. Heads have written that this is the beginning of the end of the autonomy which English schools have prized for years.

I remember one head asking, conversely, for more guidance centrally than the *Curriculum 11–16* document (1971) gave. Now, of course, local education authorities are required to draw up policy documents about the curriculum in schools. There are many fierce battles still to be fought over the implementation of any such policies. What is certain is that many headteachers will be looking to touchstones such as 'balance', 'common curriculum' and perhaps 'technical and vocational training' to help them evaluate their own school's status in the light of the demands of these policy documents.

It is my guess that one of the policy document requirements in many local education authorities will be the provision schools are making for the Personal, Social and Moral Education of their pupils. The Department of Education and Science and Her Majesty's Inspectorate of Schools documents, with their emphasis on this area of the curriculum, may be sitting in the deputy headmaster's study gathering dust, but the LEA policy documents will enshrine some of the thinking in those dusty documents which will affect every member of the staff-room. As I write this chapter, our own Bedfordshire document has been going through draft stages for discussion. It will be interesting for teachers to see what requirements are laid on their school in the future for the Personal, Social and Moral Education of their pupils.

More recently, again, the education press has been full of the news about the government's proposals through the Manpower Services Commission to exert more influence on the school curriculum. An article in *The Times Educational Supplement* indicated the government's determination to introduce vocational and practical training into the education of pupils of 14–17. Where LEAs will not comply with these wishes, the MSC has said it has the power to set up alternative schools under its own jurisdiction. The government seems determined to give young people new training opportunities, either during the latter years of their education, or when they begin the Youth Training Schemes from the age of 16.

These proposals are in part a response to the great problems of young people who leave school without the prospect of employment In my view, the school curriculum must respond to these social changes Schools in societies with high unemployment must fearlessly face the question of how they are preparing all of their pupils for their future lives. It is plainly unjust to give only a few children opportunities, skills and knowledge for the future. We must give all our pupils an effective Personal, Social and Moral Education. This, then, is the purpose of this book: to invite the reader to think again about the education we offer our young people particularly in the area of personal, social and moral dimensions of the curriculum. We invite the reader to evaluate the arguments put forward here and then boldly to relate our ideals and values to the practical situations of our schools, so that theory becomes practice and ideals become action.

Footnotes

1. D. H. Hamblin, *The Teacher and Counselling*.
2. K. David, *Pastoral Work and Education in Personal Relationships*; Reading, Berks LEA, *Who Cares?*
3. M. Marland, *Pastoral Care*; D. H. Hamblin, *The Teacher and Pastoral Care*.
4. J. Baldwin, H. Wells, *Active Tutorial Work*.
5. C. Ball, M. Ball, *Education for a Change*.

CHAPTER 2

DEFINITION AND JUSTIFICATION

What is Personal, Social and Moral Education, and how may we justify our interest in it?

Some years ago I was asked by a board of governors to go to a meeting to explain what we meant by Social Education. There had been some confusion about what it might be. Did it mean organizing trips, arranging clubs or dances for children? Did it include lunch-time activities such as chess, or football and hockey? Was it what some people call the extra-curricular activities of a school? Perhaps it might be more sinister, in the form of some sort of social engineering. Were we moulding the children into compliant factory workers or, even worse, sowing the seeds of discontent in their souls which might blossom into left-wing tendencies? What was needed then, and now, is a clarification of what we are talking about.

At my school we happen to call PSME by the umbrella term 'Social Education'. In this book we will always refer to this area of the curriculum as Personal, Social and Moral Education. When I decided to sit down and try to describe to these governors what we meant by our work, this is what I wrote: '. . . those aspects of school life which contribute to the process of growing-up, getting on with other people, the formation of values and the preparation of the child for responsibility in adult life. This includes helping pupils to understand themselves, their behaviour, health and development, and to understand our society. It includes helping children to understand their school, and to learn effectively. We teach our children how to make decisions and moral judgements; we encourage them to be sensitive to their environment and

to the beliefs and behaviour of others; and we try to foster an awareness of the major problems of mankind. Aspects of this process (PSME) are found in the home, in various lessons in the school, through the pastoral organization, and in the ways people behave toward each other in school; but we have also organized courses for each year group in which topics suitable for the age, development and interest of the pupils are explored. PSME can be in danger of becoming a subject, but we try to avoid this by balancing content with process.' This was the best description I was able to compose in the time available, and I have not changed it significantly since.

The term 'Personal, Social and Moral Education' is preferable to 'Social Education' because it describes further dimensions of the area. The *Personal* refers to the growing self-awareness of pupils, their self-esteem, understanding of the process of growing up, and awareness of their attitudes, emotions, values and beliefs. It may also include personal health.

The *Social* refers more to the place of others in the pupil's life, his relationships, his feelings about those close to him, and the way he might fit into groups of people. It includes wider issues—not only his self-consciousness in relation to others—but of his awareness and understanding of other people, the institutions of society, and the problems of both the local and wider communities. The relation of the individual to the state, concepts of a more political nature, such as use of power, government, beliefs about how society should be organized, the place of law, police, crime and punishment—all these are what I loosely term 'social'. At one time we

used to call this 'education for citizenship'. The world of work, the production of wealth, the preparation of children for adult roles which has been denoted 'Careers Education' in England, comes under this umbrella, 'social'.

The *Moral* has more to do with the way an individual behaves towards others. It is concerned with questions of 'ought' and 'should', of 'duty', and about principles which regulate the private lives of individuals. It is about the principles by which I arrive at my behaviour. Judgements about right and wrong, about the nature of virtue or the good life, and how best to practise it—these are ethical or moral concerns. Moral Education is that part of PSME which helps the young person to understand what moral questions are about, how to recognize moral issues, how to arrive at a moral decision. Moral Education is the consideration of principles and codes of moral life and reading examples of the moral life proposed by great men and women. It includes the reading of accounts of people exemplifying what might be considered as the 'good life'. Moral Education consists not simply of teaching moral reasoning, but also of encouraging young people to practise their principles. Further, I believe a school has a duty to inculcate virtues which it considers pre-eminent. I shall discuss this in more detail later.

PSME cannot be limited to one subject. We are talking about realms of experience here, dimensions of the whole curriculum and what has been called the hidden curriculum. All that the school plans, organizes and implements contributes to the PSME of the pupils. The unintended as well as the intended, as David Hargreaves illustrates so well,[1] contributes to the PSME of the pupil.

I return again in later chapters to the importance of the hidden values of a school, and how critical it is that headteachers and managers in schools are constantly vigilant, attentive to creating a match between their stated values and this more elusive but equally powerful and influential area of the hidden curriculum. A whole curriculum view of PSME is likely to be more effective if it can be achieved, rather than stating intentions, or through a splintered approach by individual subjects.

I am well aware that my attempts to clarify PSME to my governors, and the paragraphs above, may raise problems for the philosopher of education. But I hope that the ordinary teacher may be a little clearer about what I mean by PSME.

A philosopher of education who has contributed much practical help to this area is Richard Pring of Exeter University. He combines the philosophical skills of analysis with a rich practical experience of PSME, in both the UK and USA. Professor Pring was a member of the panel on Personal and Social Development of the Assessment and Performance Unit of the Department of Education and Science in England. The APU decided to investigate the desirability and feasibility of monitoring this aspect of children's development. The exploratory team panel was asked to make a comprehensive survey of the whole area under consideration, but after four years' work no satisfactory way round the difficulties inherent in proposals for assessment in this area were found, so the APU did not proceed with a national programme of monitoring children's PSM development.

Despite the considerable importance attached to personal and social development by a large body of the community, it is not an easy area to describe . . . In one sense, everything a person knows, understands, feels and does is part of his or her personal and social development . . . The first major task of the group was to

PERSONAL AND SOCIAL DEVELOPMENT

HOME	SCHOOL	WIDER COMMUNITY

SCHOOL VALUE SYSTEM	CURRICULUM	PASTORAL CARE

● explicit
● implicit
● rituals
● relationships
● groupings
● organization
● curriculum on offer
● rules
● pupil value system
	● contribution of
	  methods
	  materials
	  relationships
	● English
	● Humanities
	● Science
	● Religious Education
	● Moral Education
	● Health Education
	● Physical Education
	● Careers Education
	● Home Studies
	● Social Sciences
	● Mathematics
	● Art and Design
	● Creative and
	Expressive Arts
	● Technical Studies
	● Special courses
	  Parentcraft
	  Social Education
		● Purpose?
		  control
		  learning environment
		  administration
		  counselling
		  guidance
		● Underlying values
		● Organization
		● Person- or
		institution-centred?
		● Pastoral Curriculum?
		● Role of form tutors?

PUPIL

PERSONAL AND SOCIAL DEVELOPMENT: MAP OF THE TERRITORY

Aspects of development	Dimensions			
	Knowledge	Understanding	Practical application	Attitudes
a. General development				
Persons and personal relationships				
Morality				
Social awareness				
b. Religion, philosophies of life				
c. Specific development:				
Occupational				
Political				
Legal				
Environmental				
Health				
Community				

From *Personal and Social Development*, APU Report, DES 1981

'map the territory' as an essential preliminary . . .

The group concluded that personal and social development could be broken down into a series of aspects and dimensions. Aspects of *general development* concerned with persons and personal relationships, morality and social awareness and aspects of *specific development* concerned with occupational, political, legal, environmental, health and community areas.

These were seen as common to each aspect of development, viz: a. knowledge b. understanding c. practical application d. attitudes. The Group's final map of the territory can be expressed as a grid, representing in its vertical axes the general and specific aspects of personal and social development and in its horizontal axes, knowledge, understanding, practical application and attitudes.[2]

From *Personal and Social Development*, APU Report, DES 1981 (italics mine)

The APU report talks about two aspects, the general and the specific. These are helpful in getting to grips with understanding and clarifying what is meant by PSME, and in planning principles for the curriculum. The general aspect is that which influences our life as a whole in the realm of knowing, understanding, believing, in the area of personal and social development. They are general because they are not specific to a subject, but affected by the influence of home, social, cultural and ethnic differences. The specific developments may derive from general developments, but the individual is called upon to display practical skills or knowledge in particular contexts. These aspects may coincide with particular subjects or areas of the curriculum. Religion and philosophies of life could fit into either of these, so they were dealt with as a separate category. The report goes on to give examples of categories of knowledge, understanding, and so on, in each of the aspects of development. I will return to these later.

Richard Pring has obviously continued to reflect on 'mapping the territory'. In *The Cambridge Journal of Education* (Vol. 12, No. 1, Lent Term, 1982), which contains a series of articles proceeding from the Cambridge Conference, 'Curriculum Planning for Personal and Social Development', he makes the distinction about development *as a person* and development *as a person of a certain sort*. His matrix for planning, which we shall look at later, is a development of the original map.

What at least is apparent from what I have said is the complexity of the area. As a start to curriculum planning there is a need to sort out this complexity into some sort of coherent map of the territory that respects the various distinctions I have made. This, however, can be no more than a sort of check-list, a guide to school-based curriculum discussion and planning. *Remember first that PSD comprises the development of qualities essential to being a person as well as qualities of being a person of a certain sort . . . Remember secondly that PSD is concerned not only with the development of consciousness in its various forms, but also with the feelings, emotions, dispositions on the one hand and with particular behaviours, skills, and habits on the other.*

Richard Pring (italics mine)

Some teachers find the philosophical contributions a hindrance rather than a help to the discussion, but I think the work of the APU and of Pring do help to make clearer what we are talking about when we use expressions such as Personal, Social and Moral Education. There are several check-lists of the area in existence, some describing aspects of PSME from which aims may be derived, and some rather more like lists of content. What perhaps is a more searching question, and certainly more important, is 'What kind of PSME are we offering in our schools?'

As I shall argue later, PSME is not value free. We may have particular views about what kinds of people our school should be producing. We may have a view of society that education should work towards. Teachers often foster qualities of obedience, conformity, co-operation and compliance, even though they claim to aim at autonomy, individuality, independence and initiative in their pupils' education. The methods they adopt in teaching, the arrangement of the class-room, and perhaps the learning materials they use, all have hidden messages and in-built value assumptions. We shall return to these issues in a later chapter.

What of the second question posed at the beginning of this chapter? What is the justification for Personal, Social and Moral Education? Why should schools include PSME in the curriculum? What answer can we give to those who say that these dimensions of human experience are best left to the home, church, or to another aspect of community life such as special classes run by community leaders outside of school time?

In principle I have no objection to arrangements for PSME outside the curriculum. Indeed it is probably most effective and powerful in the family, through the teaching of the church, or by community leaders in village life, where there is agreement about what counts as values and accepted behaviour. However, what of the society which has pluralism of values, where there are no agreed codes of behaviour, where the family is becoming an unstable unit? What of the society where city life has led to the decay of communities and given rise to dehumanized values, crime, violent behaviour, or low community morale due to poor housing conditions or high unemployment? Has the school anything to offer children in the way of promoting healthy self-esteem, in raising vision to improve the quality of life, in inculcating responsibility, or encouraging collaboration over attempts to solve problems in the local community? Should not a school have some contribution to make to the pupil's understanding of what might constitute the nature of the 'good' or moral life?

In the reality of day-to-day life in schools it is not possible to avoid judgements about what is good or bad behaviour. Teachers are requently heard talking about the conduct of their pupils, about the dispositions, virtues, character traits, personal values, and social competences of their children. They speak disapprovingly of some, and actively encourage others. A school has social, moral, political, and aesthetic values built into the organization, the philosophy of the school, the teaching methods, what is expected of the pupils, and what the school offers as a curriculum.

Recently, at my own school in Luton, we have been going through the process of questioning whether there is a match between what we profess as our values and what we actually do. We have been teasing out whether our explicit values and philosophy, which is written in the staff handbook and underlies the speeches to parents on open evenings, are matched by what we do in the school, the implicit values embodied in our practice. I believe that a school by its very nature and practice is involved in the personal, social and moral aspects of education, even if subjects of that name or inquiries into these areas do not appear openly on the school timetable.

I have visited various schools in Austria where terms such as 'pastoral curriculum', 'moral education', 'religious education', 'human development', or 'values education' may not be understood, may not appear in a director's description of what goes on in the school, may even be forbidden by custom agreement or by law, but I was nevertheless able to detect PSME elements in the atmosphere and practice of the school. I visited one school where religion gave an underlying ruling to relationships, a kind of tinting to the social spectacles through which pupils saw each other, the staff and visitors. Even the common social greeting had an old religious connotation. One school, where they specialized in expressive arts, music and painting, had a sense of individual freedom, a creative atmosphere for the students. In another school a different kind of control was evident. There was a deference to authority, a conformity to the expected behaviour, a

compliance in the orderly way people moved about the building, attended in class, and waited quietly around the machinery in the workshops. In another institution there was a gaiety, a warmth, a relaxed atmosphere about the building. I noticed that our host had a lively, accepting and personal quality in his relationship with many of his students. There was a lot of laughter, smiles and natural, warm, family

---

'We, as adults, parents, teachers or whatever our relationship with young people may be, are involved in moral education, in passing on values, in helping or not helping our children to find and apply solutions to their interpersonal problems whether we like it or not, whether we accept the role or not. By what we are, or are not, by what we do or fail to do, by what we profess or do not profess, we educate boys and girls in behaviour through our everyday unselfconscious contacts with them. It is, we submit, better to know what is happening, to understand what we adults are doing to the young or are failing to do for them, than to let it all happen in ignorance while deluding ourselves that we are minding our own business, are not interfering with the "natural" development of individuals.'[3]
P. McPhail, J. R. Ungoed-Thomas and Hilary Chapman, *Moral Education in the Secondary School*, 1972

---

elements in what I observed in the class-room and over a meal.

These differences in the school ethos, in teacher-pupil relationships, in the social organization, in pupil behaviour, which are noticed by people who visit many schools, display hidden principles, values, and philosophy. A visitor may not notice everything. There may be special shows for the day, or he may take away a wrong impression, but an observer can detect different emphases in schools on the personal, social and moral development of their students. Indeed, within one school it is possible to observe striking differences in the way that individual teachers are educating their pupils.

The quotation above summarizes the argument of these paragraphs.

What the authors say about the moral dimension is, I believe, equally true of the personal and social. I believe a school should grasp this wild, rambling and thorny briar, cut it down to some manageable proportion, and then graft and prune the rose to produce the blooms which the community desires.

The question, 'How do we arrive at the school curriculum?', has engaged the minds of the philosophers of education for many years. In England, teachers dip into the writings of Richard Peters and Paul Hirst in their initial training, but I have found them to be suspicious of or impatient with philosophical arguments while they have the pressing demands of class-rooms on their minds. Yet the questions of 'justification' are very important. Why do we teach Bach but not bingo, history but not hunting and fishing, science but not survival? School subjects, as we have them, may not have sacrosanct, logical or psychological justifications. Most of us accept the subjects and teach them because we were trained in them, or because examination boards set papers in those subjects. Pupils, however, do not always see why they should study these particular subjects.

The thesis that knowledge, understanding and human meanings consist of a limited number of different kinds has captivated philosophers and epistemologists since the time of Plato. Thinkers in education come up with various arrangements of the thesis. Paul Hirst writes about the various forms of knowledge which develop the essential distinguishing characteristic of mankind which he claims is 'mind'. Education, he argues, should derive from the nature of knowledge itself and not from the whims of politicians, the demands of a capitalist society, or just the interests of the pupils. He claims in his essay 'Liberal Education and the Nature of Knowledge'[4] that there are distinctive forms of knowledge, or disciplines, which are unique ways of understanding experience.

Philip Phenix maintains in *Realms of Meaning*[5] that there are six 'fundamental patterns of meaning which emerge from the analysis of possible distinctive modes of human understanding'. He believes that, because they determine the quality of significant experience, a general education should comprise these basic realms to develop a whole person. The reader who is interested in these philosophical arguments can pursue them by reading the references listed at the end of the chapter, or by reading Richard Pring's excellent introduction (and critique of the differentiated curriculum) in *Knowledge and Schooling*.[6]

The HMI (Her Majesty's Inspectorate) of Schools document *Curriculum 11–16* has defined what it calls essential areas of experience which should be the central concerns of the school curriculum in England. These are the aesthetic and creative, the ethical, the linguistic, the mathematical, the physical, the scientific, the social and political, and the spiritual. It makes the point that none of these areas of experience can be equated with one subject.

There has been criticism that human experience is not reducible to Hirst's, Phenix's or even the HMI lists of forms, realms, or areas of experience. Hirst's writing has been used to bolster the academic, cerebral curriculum, and the HMI list seems to be developing into the new orthodoxy. However, what concerns us here is that the area of Personal, Social and Moral Education has been identified in various guises as essential to the curriculum in these philosophical discussions.

Hirst talks about moral knowledge, philosophy, human sciences, literature, arts. Phenix talks about Empirics, which embraces psychology and social sciences as well as physical sciences, Esthetics, which includes a lot of personal development, and Synnoetics, which covers many aspects of PSME (as I have described it), such as philosophy, psychology, literature, religion. He denotes two further areas or realms—Ethics and Synoptics—which are the special area of moral concern and history, religion and philosophy. The HMI document gives much weight to our justification for PSME in their eight

categories, particularly in the aesthetic, ethical, social and political and spiritual areas.

What I am claiming, therefore, is that there are good philosophical grounds for arguing that PSME should be part of the school curriculum. If we claim to derive our curriculum from the nature of knowledge, realms of meaning, or from essential human experiences, it must include the personal, the social and the moral dimensions.

Further, there are strong psychological reasons for PSME. There is a view of the process of education as a 'shopping trolley model', where the child consumer walks through the supermarket school picking up packages of knowledge, the check-out being some kind of examination system. The trouble is, of course, that many of our youngsters either do not possess the right currency to get through the check-out, or else cannot see the point of it all. How often do we hear the whine, 'why do we have to learn this?', or 'this is so boring', from our pupils? I am not too happy about giving such justifications as, 'because it's on the exam syllabus', or 'because if you don't pass this exam you won't get the job you want'. These justifications sound increasingly hollow in countries of high unemployment.

I believe what is needed is a curriculum with which children will gladly identify. Our youngsters need to see the point of their lessons in terms of their own growing self-awareness, their own consciousness of the world. There needs to be a *psychological validity* about our work in school. I want those packages of knowledge out there to be possessed by the pupils not only as external bodies of knowledge, but as insights, skills, concepts—knowledge which helps them interpret the world and their own experience. I want children to be partners in learning, not compliant receivers of facts. This interaction of the child's mind and experience with new knowledge, skills and experience will lead to further development of the minds of the children. I am not denying the need for disciplined hard work in the class-room, nor for the learning of

essential processes, rules, facts and skills from which the learner may proceed further in his understanding. However, there must also be the capturing of the child's imagination, his search for knowledge, the arousing of curiosity, the fostering of strong motivation, if the child is to understand what he is doing. It is a sad reflection on so much of what we do in secondary schools that our children may fill their memories with our lessons, then leave the class-room shrugging their shoulders, with a 'so what?' look or comment.

This is, of course, a much wider issue, but I believe PSME can help in this debate about psychological validity for the child, what we used to call 'relevance' in the child-centred training colleges of the 1960s. If a school takes the dimensions of Personal, Social and Moral Education seriously in constructing a curriculum, the child is fairly central to it. PSME is about the child emerging from adolescence into adulthood. It is about his self-esteem, his growing awareness of his opinions, beliefs and values. It is about his relationships with people, his learning to relate to different adults who have a wide variety of expectations of him. It is about his coming to terms with authority, with developing independence, with responsibility. PSME is about a girl's growing awareness of her womanhood, about learning to cope with her emotions, about learning to express her new awareness through clothes and fashion. Young people begin to work out for themselves questions of duty, of what is right and wrong. They are exploring worlds of meaning because they want to make sense of the present and fill their vision with ideals for their future. The excitement of sexual awareness, of the prospect of earning a wage, of becoming independent of parents, often brings new anxieties and uncertainties, and perhaps a challenge to parental values.

Surely a school curriculum which ignores these factors is providing an inadequate education in things which really matter to young people? The content of conversations in corridors, the illicit notes passed from Susie to Sam, the arguments that develop

The personal dimension and social relationships are vitally important to children.

tween twelve-year-old girls who l out with each other and then are som comrades twice in a week—all ustrate the importance of the rsonal dimension and of social ationships to children. Indeed, ter Wood's research indicates that en children become alienated from e aims of the school curriculum it their own substitute social and rsonal interests which sustain em.[7]

In reality, schools cannot avoid the ychological need boys and girls ve for their interests, development, rsonal values and behaviour to be en some account of. Teachers may el PSME is an inappropriate rusion into more important ademic concerns—and then along mes Mohammed, late for his son because he has been bullied in e toilets. We cannot pretend ationship problems between chers and pupils do not exist in glish comprehensive schools, nor we ignore the moods of Jenny o has just been jilted by John. e way Jenny is feeling affects her rk. I believe that a school needs to

have not only academic disciplines, technical skills and intellectual and creative experiences at the centre of its work, but that the personal, social and moral needs of the child should never be far from our minds.

There needs to be a psychological validity for the children in our work in schools which meets their needs, which consults them about what they want to know. A programme of Personal, Social and Moral Education will help to ensure this validity of education in the minds of the young if it fulfils the criteria I have been describing—that is, if they identify and co-operate with, and are personally involved in, their learning—and secondly if the curriculum meets their living minds and experience and their current needs. The psychological justification for Personal, Social and Moral Education is that it is valid in the minds of the pupils because it is concerned with young people's understanding of themselves, with their relationships, their community problems, and their future.

My next few paragraphs may be

more controversial, because I want to make a case, on social and political grounds, for including the dimension of PSME in our school curriculum. This need not necessarily be as a subject, but as an infusion into the life of the school or, to change the analogy, as threads in the warp and woof of the philosophy, organized curriculum, and wider life of the school.

If social education 'passes on to those living in a society the traditions, practices and rules that govern behaviour in that society', as Peter McPhail suggests in one of his books,[8] surely there will be what may be termed social or political concepts, practices or ideals which a school may wish to transmit. Take, for example, the notion of democracy, or the ideals enshrined in the constitution of the United States of America, or the principles in the Declaration of Human Rights in the

United Nations Charter. These political and social aspects of PSME might be considered essential to the education of the young in a particular country. Loyalty to the flag, the freedom of the individual, the importance of choice based on an understanding of alternatives, might also be elements of political and social education. Presumably a state school, in whatever country, has a duty to inculcate respect for the law, because just law may be considered to be the foundation of civilized societies.

The danger of political and social education is that one political party may wish the schools to indoctrinate or manipulate the minds of the young, as happened in Nazi Germany, 1939–45. Perhaps schools must always balance their wish to inculcate social or political values, however noble, with the notion of respect for persons. It appears there must always be a tension between the desire to protect the individual's right to make personal decisions and the need for transmitting the values and traditions of our forefathers. Perhaps PSME can provide a forum in schools where these tensions can be experienced and explored by the young. Another strong tension is the conflict between individualism and the need for a common vision of the kind of society we want in the future. David Hargreaves writes a critique of individualism and argues for the restoration of community values in his book *The Challenge for The Comprehensive School*, which I found stimulating reading.

I believe we need social and political dimensions to Personal, Social and Moral Education in spite of the risks of indoctrination from either the Communist left or the extreme Fascist right, in countries where there is political and economic instability. It seems to me that the directors, governors, local community leaders, together with teachers, parents and other interested parties, need to think hard about what they wish to preserve and transmit from the past and present. Then we need to ascertain what might need changing, or what problems need attention in community life. These aims may be

plotted on a continuum from reproductive and conservative on the right, through to change and radical on the left. There is also another continuum, that of whether we should be educating for autonomy, individualism, and independence of mind and values, or whether we should sink our individualism for the common good and educate for co-operation, collaborative action, and community life.

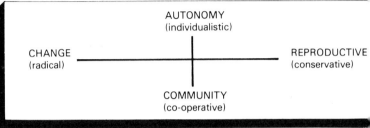

It would be very foolish to assert that progress is straightforward in such a notoriously controversial area. I offer this diagram only as a possible tool for working out a community's aims for social and political education. Teachers cannot avoid the political and social implications of their work. A school which does not, to some extent, prepare its students for adult roles in society, is lacking in its vision. A society needs young people who are aware of the strengths and weaknesses of that society. It needs some young people who will be willing to work at the problems, preserve the best of our past, and care enough about injustices to try to change them. The school must have a function in arousing these interests, equipping young people with necessary knowledge and skills. Without a vision for the future in our schools, community life and personal values may decay further. A school's vision for the future will include political and social values.

Finally, in this section on the justification for Personal, Social and Moral Education, I want to argue that on moral or spiritual grounds it is essential that we have curriculum planning in this area. I have already discussed the growth of personal values and beliefs as an important process in the development of the individual, whether from a

psychological viewpoint or from a moral/spiritual perspective. Schools should be helping young people to develop personal values and community values, as I have said earlier. Moral and spiritual beliefs underpin and determine much of what we think and the way we behave, how we view life and other people. McPhail and others in *Moral Education in the Secondary School* found from their empirical evidence,

their surveys of the problems and opinions of girls and boys, that young people were intensely interested in human relations, and in instances of goodness and badness. The Schools Council Project *Lifeline* built its theory of morals on this evidence, 'concern for one another's needs, interests and feelings as well as one's own . . .' Ten years later McPhail writes (italics mine): 'In this book I invite you to consider the ways in which children and young people learn how to treat individuals, animals, other forms of life, the earth and the objects with which men surround themselves. There is no more important subject of study than this process and the part we play in it. *The future of the world depends, quite literally, on what we find out and on what action we take.*'[9]

Some readers may feel McPhail is making exaggerated claims. But in Britain the threat of a nuclear holocaust feels very real to the women who are protesting about the basing of Cruise missiles in the Berkshire countryside. The 80-year-old woman who was raped by a 14-year-old lad might have strong feelings about the moral education of the young. The victims of muggings (a word I had not heard of in my teenage years), might have strong opinions about the place of moral education in schools.

If we take a calmer, more rational

approach to the area—even a cold, statistical one—there are social trends which dismay even the stout-hearted. Family life, which was considered the basic unit of society for the reproduction of our species, for the care, protection and socialization of the young in earlier textbooks on sociology, is now under threat. One in three marriages in Britain ends in divorce, we are told. Schoolteachers, social workers and policemen see the trauma and emotional damage in all but the most resilient children when family life is disturbed. I hesitate to talk of social changes in what might appear an alarmist way, but there are undoubtedly major changes in employment, acceptance of authority, and in agreed values about what counts as right and wrong in a pluralistic, multi-cultural society.

The preliminary study from the 1981 Schools Council Lifeline research quoted by McPhail notes that there have been changes among young people in the UK since the 1960s. Children tend now to treat others in the way they are treated. There is an increase in aggression and physical violence, and some evidence of an increase in psychological cruelty. There is a growing resentment of immigrant groups. There is resentment against the government, particularly with regard to unemployment. There appears to be more boredom and lack of challenge. McPhail's chapter on the future of social and moral education is challenging reading: 'Some of the statistics could lead us to accept that only an incorrigible optimist would devote his life to social and moral education. For example, 50% of the world's scientists and engineers are involved in military research and development. In poorer parts of the world five times more money is spent on arms than on agricultural machinery. More than 12 million children die each year before they reach the age of 5. Killer diseases, such as malaria, typhoid and sleeping sickness, could be eradicated for half what is spent in one year on military resources. One could continue in this vein almost indefinitely.'[10]

Moralists, sociologists, school-teachers, would all add their own particular flavour to the moral problems in society today. I have no doubt that all that is said about Britain could also be said about the USA—perhaps more so. What of other countries? I have little personal knowledge, but I ask the reader: What concerns you about the principles and behaviour that individuals are taught in your schools? Are you happy with the principles that govern and regulate the private and social lives of people in your society?

I believe there is an urgent need for teachers to consider the implications of the moral education their pupils are receiving. Are there basic principles of freedom, justice, respect for persons which are the ground rules for moral life? How should we help children think about principles of behaviour and personal relationships? Is it enough to teach moral reasoning and not concern ourselves with moral action? I shall return to these questions later, when I discuss the distinctive contribution of the Christian to moral education in our schools.

In this chapter I have tried to clarify what I mean by the personal, the social and moral aspects of education. Readers will readily recognize that there are personal, social and moral dimensions to many of the traditional subjects, such as Geography, Biology, History, and more obviously in Art, Literature, Music, Religion and social sciences. Later, in another chapter, I want to argue that a piecemeal, splintered approach to Personal, Social and Moral Development is less effective than the planned, co-ordinated whole-curriculum approach.

I have also selected some reasons to justify the importance of this area of the curriculum. What I have said could be adapted to youth work situations with similar justifications. I could equally well have referred to the writings about Health Education,[11] to the arguments of the pastoral care movement in British schools,[12] or to the American humanistic educators, such as C. Rogers.

Although I have written from the context of English schools, I believe the four main arguments I have selected for the justification of Personal, Social and Moral Education can be related to other educational systems. Are there any grounds for argument that could possibly be important or strong enough to suggest that PSME should be excluded from the school curriculum in any country? Can we possibly afford to leave out these dimensions of the curriculum? In reality do we leave out these areas in our day-to-day work with girls and boys?

'It is well known that school transforms the identities of many of the children: transforms the nature of their allegiances to their family and community, and gives them access to other styles of life and modes of social relationships.'
Basil Bernstein, *Class, Codes and Control*

The personal, social and moral development of our children is far too important to be left to accident, haphazard or poorly planned programmes of teaching. We need carefully constructed aims and sound planning principles, together with co-ordinated programmes of work for our young people.

Footnotes

1. D. Hargreaves, *The Challenge for the Comprehensive School*, Ch.1.
2. *Personal and Social Development*.
3. McPhail et al, *Moral Education in the Secondary School*, pp. 11–12.
4. P. Hirst, *Knowledge and the Curriculum*.
5. P. Phenix, *Realms of Meaning*.
6. R. Pring, *Knowledge and Schooling*.
7. P. Woods, M. Hammersley, 'Having a Laugh' in *The Process of Schooling*.
8. P. McPhail, *Social and Moral Education*.
9. P. McPhail, *Social and Moral Education*, p.1.
10. P. McPhail, *Social and Moral Education*, p.191.
11. See Discussion Paper No. 8, *Health Education*.
12. See, for example, the writings of Douglas Hamblin or Ken David.

CHAPTER 3

THE QUESTION OF VALUES

I believe that Personal, Social and Moral Education is not and cannot be value free. R. S. Peters says: '"Education" has notions such as "improvement", "betterment" and "the passing on of what is worth while" built into it. That education must involve something of ethical value is, therefore, a matter of logical necessity.'[1]

David Bridges and Peter Scrimshaw argue that teaching involves moral issues, because what teachers do affects the future of the young. Even the practical decisions on the class-room level '. . . about the content and methods of teaching to be used, discussion at the staff-room level about assessment methods, the involvement of parents or pupils in the running of the school; all these may (and frequently do) have a moral dimension which cannot be honestly ignored, once it has been pointed out.'[2]

If this is true about the wider field of education, it is certainly true about the segment of Personal, Social and Moral Education. The central thesis of this chapter is that all approaches to PSME have value assumptions built into both the theoretical and practical aspects of the work, or they have values underlying the use of the teaching method and materials.

What do I mean by value assumptions? At my own school we had a staff conference on the values of the school. In a paper for discussion I wrote that 'a value may be conceived as an object, an idea, a principle or a system which a person or a group holds to have particular worth. A value is a standard of worth ascribed to activities, actions, behaviours, precepts, processes, and arrangements in a school'. I argued that values are an unavoidable issue in education. At almost every point

values and beliefs underlie our practice.

Our discussions took us into opposing camps about values. Some held that values are objective, that the good or value is independent of the observer, and only discovered by the mind sensitive to them. Others held the view that values are constituted by feelings, desires or expressions of approval, which rest not in the object but in the person who judges. Whatever view we take, we do bring our values into the opinions we hold about how we feel children should behave, in making decisions about the extent to which children should decide what subjects they take at fourteen or fifteen. Our value assumptions are the ground of our beliefs about the use of corporal punishment, the philosophical or faith basis which is taken for granted when we describe ideals such as wanting our pupils to have self-confidence, self-respect, and respect for others. Our value assumptions are often not made explicit. They are rather like the deep concrete piles sunk into the underlying rock of the building I have watched take shape over several months near where I live. They form the hidden foundations of the elegant steel, concrete and glass office block now visible above ground.

Some years ago, when my wife and I were first thinking of buying a home, I was attracted by a house in a pleasant neighbourhood on offer at a comparatively low price. I happened by chance to ask a friend who was a builder what he thought of this estate, and he reacted with a firm, 'Don't buy it.' 'Why not?' I asked, a little hurt. 'Because they're suspect. They have substandard foundations—only three inches of concrete,' he said. It is the foundations of the systems, methods and materials in Personal, Social and Moral Education which I want to uncover in this chapter, because there is a sense in which they too may be 'suspect'.

Teachers and youth workers who have little time for armchair reflection about the underlying values or philosophical assumptions of class-room materials such as textbooks, worksheets, tapes, videos, or films may not be aware of the implications of these materials. The unwary teacher buying a class set of books about puberty and adolescent behaviour, or hiring a film on the changes associated with adolescence in girls and boys, may, for example, find when he comes to use them that the material is slanted in a particular way, betraying the author's or publisher's assumptions about sex

'The trouble with the "new" moral education, according to Kathleen Gow, is that it is actually amoral education. Under the guise of impartiality, non-directiveness, non-indoctrination and non-interference in the child's moral autonomy, M.V.E. (moral values education) is in fact inculcating its own value perspective. What looks like a liberal tolerance of conflicting opinions is, in practice, education in moral relativism and individual utilitarianism. And this particular hidden curriculum is not only socially undesirable and at variance with our cultural tradition; it is not what most parents want for their children . . .'
Don Locke, review article of *Yes, Virginia, there is Right and Wrong*, by Kathleen Gow, 1980, in *Journal of Moral Education*, Vol. 11 No. 1, pp. 61–64

before marriage. To take another example, some newly published guides to work in tutorial periods may appear to be the panacea for all form-teacher problems. However, on closer examination, the underlying value assumptions might be highly egocentric, challenging authority, and subversive of the school.

I was first introduced to Values Clarification through the writing of Dr Sidney Simon.[3] These strategies help people to clarify their values, help them to work out what they feel, believe and prize in the controversial area of human values, especially where there is no clear agreement in society at large. We have used Values Clarification materials quite extensively in my own school. I have used the

CLARIFYING RESPONSES SUGGESTED BY THE SEVEN VALUING PROCESSES

1. Choosing freely
a. Where do you suppose you first got that idea?
b. How long have you felt that way?
c. What would people say if you weren't to do what you say you must do?
d. Are you getting help from anyone? Do you need more help? Can I help?
e. Are you the only one in your crowd who feels this way?
f. What do your parents want you to be?
g. Is there any rebellion in your choice?
h. How many years will you give to it? What will you do if you're not good enough?
i. Do you think the idea of having thousands of people cheering when you come out on the field has anything to do with your choice?

2. Choosing from alternatives
a. What else did you consider before you picked this?
b. How long did you look around before you decided?
c. Was it a hard decision? What went into the final decision? Who helped? Do you need any further help?
d. Did you consider another possible alternative?
e. Are there some reasons behind your choice?
f. What choices did you reject before you settled on your present idea or action?
g. What's really good about this choice which makes it stand out from the other possibilities?

3. Choosing thoughtfully and reflectively
a. What would be the consequences of each alternative available?
b. Have you thought about this very much? How did your thinking go?

c. Is this what I understand you to say . . . (interpret statement)?
d. Are you implying that . . . (distort statement to see if the student is clear enough to correct the distortion)?
e. What assumptions are involved in your choice? Let's examine them.
f. Define the terms you use. Give me an example of the kind of job you can get without a high-school diploma.
g. Now if you do this, what will happen to that . . .?
h. Is what you say consistent with what you said earlier?
i. Just what is good about this choice?
j. Where will it lead?
k. For whom are you doing this?
l. With these other choices, rank them in order of significance.
m. What will you have to do? What are your first steps? Second steps?
n. Whom else did you talk to?
o. Have you really weighed it fully?

4. Prizing and cherishing
a. Are you glad you feel that way?
b. How long have you wanted it?
c. What good is it? What purpose does it serve? Why is it important to you?
d. Should everyone do it your way?
e. Is it something you really prize?
f. In what way would life be different without it?

5. Affirming
a. Would you tell the class the way you feel some time?
b. Would you be willing to sign a petition supporting that idea?
c. Are you saying that you believe . . . (repeat the idea)?
d. You don't mean to say that you believe . . . (repeat the idea)?
e. Should a person who believes the way you do speak out?
f. Do people know that you believe that way or that you do that thing?
g. Are you willing to stand up and be counted for that?

6. Acting upon choices
a. I hear what you are for; now, is there anything you can do about it? Can I help?
b. What are your first steps, second steps, etc.?
c. Are you willing to put some of your money behind this idea?
d. Have you examined the consequences of your act?
e. Are there any organizations set up for the same purposes? Will you join?
f. Have you done much reading on the topic? Who has influenced you?
g. Have you made any plans to do more than you already have done?
h. Would you want other people to know you feel this way? What if they disagree with you?
i. Where will this lead you? How far are you willing to go?
j. How has it already affected your life? How will it affect it in the future?

7. Repeating
a. Have you felt this way for some time?
b. Have you done anything already? Do you do this often?
c. What are your plans for doing more of it?
d. Should you get other people interested and involved?
e. Has it been worth the time and money?
f. Are there some other things you can do which are like it?
g. How long do you think you will continue?
h. What did you *not* do when you went to do that? Was that all right?

Reproduced from L. Raths, M. Harmin, S. Simons, *Values and Teaching*, pp. 64–65, 1978

technique which the approach adopts successfully in the class-room, with full class groups and with small discussion groups, and also in a church youth group.

I want to go back to the original sources so that the reader is presented with a more faithful account of Values Clarification. In describing how this approach to PSME developed, L. Raths, M. Harmin and S. Simon[4] relate how the Supreme Court ruling that common prayer should not be demanded of all children in schools in the USA led teachers to turn towards 'teaching the facts', avoiding controversy. It also led to administrators preferring teachers who did not raise 'issues'. They say that, 'Moral, ethical, aesthetic values were quietly abandoned as integral parts of the curriculum.'

The authors succinctly describe the causes of concern in society in the 1960s and go on to underline their concerns about violence, corruption in high places, the aftermath of the

How can our wonderful channels of communication be used to help people see the alternatives that lie before us and see them clearly? How can we be helped to see the consequences that may flow from each alternative available? How may we see more clearly the resources we have for attacking these most serious problems of our society? And, finally, how may we be helped to choose priorities?

We thought in 1965 that there was a most serious need for more methods to help clarify the purposes and aspirations, the interests and attitudes, the beliefs and activities of young people in the schools of America. Our book was widely acclaimed and has been used in hundreds upon hundreds of schools and school districts. Now in 1978 we are only able to say that the need is even greater than it was a decade ago.

From the Introduction, *Values and Teaching*

Vietnam War, racial conflict and drug abuse in the 1970s. The Values Clarification strategies were designed in response, therefore, to the problems in society and to the gap left in the school curriculum by the interpretations of the Supreme Court decision in the USA. What, then, did they mean by Values Clarification?

The authors are interested in the process of valuing, of making decisions. They want children to re-

create values continuously, rather than standing dreary guard over ancient values. They want 'to give children a process of valuing that should serve them well and long'. They see values as growing from experience, modified, changing, maturing over time. They believe humans arrive at values by seven processes:

- choosing freely
- choosing from alternatives
- choosing having considered the consequences of each alternative
- prizing by cherishing and being happy with their choice
- being bold enough to affirm their choice to others
- acting or doing as a result of the choice
- repeating the action in some pattern of life.

Choosing, prizing and acting are the key processes. The authors claim that our values are what we arrive at by this intelligent process. They admit that there are purposes, aspirations and beliefs which may not fulfil all seven of their criteria. These are not values in their sense. Goals, aspirations, attitudes, interests, feelings, beliefs and convictions, activities, worries, problems and obstacles may lead to values. In summary, these authors believe that if people are to develop values they must 'develop them out of personal choice'. Values, they believe, are a product of personal experience, not just a matter of 'true' or 'false'. The clarification process takes place by helping young people to use the seven processes.

At this point the reader may be asking questions. What about

DO YOU

1. feel that the news media (TV, newspapers, etc.) generally distort the truth?

2. approve of a six month to a year trial marriage?

3. believe that today's young generation is more open and honest than the older generation is?

4. feel that self-discipline is better than imposed discipline?

5. like the idea of creating your own school curriculum rather than having school administrators do it?

6. frown upon people who resort frequently to four-letter words in their conversation?

7. think that physical punishment is sometimes a necessary disciplinary tactic?

8. feel free to discuss personal problems with your parents and friends?

9. value friendship above economic success?

10. have discriminating tastes in terms of the TV programs you watch?

11. think that violence on TV encourages violence in the street?

12. subscribe to a weekly news magazine and read it faithfully?

13. enjoy entertaining friends at your home?

14. like to eat at expensive restaurants?

15. worry about your financial security?

16. have rather high ambitions for your future?

17. enjoy spending time with your family?

From S. Simon, *Meeting Yourself Halfway*

bjectivity in values? Are values only my feelings about objects? Are statements of value only statements about the emotional state of the speaker? Are there not beliefs, practices, values which are worth transmitting to succeeding generations and 'standing cherished and active guard' because they *merit* our approval?

I have no doubt about the effectiveness of Values Clarification strategies. However, I do have reservations about some of the authors' assumptions and about the philosophical foundations on which the authors base their writing.

One assumption is that other approaches to values education have not worked as well as was hoped. They list eight examples of such methods:

- the setting of an example
- persuading and convincing
- limiting choices
- inspiring by emotional pleas
- rules and regulations which contain and mould behaviour
- the use of arts and literature to expand awareness and promote values
- the presentation of cultural or religious dogma
- appeals to conscience.

They assert that these cannot lead to values in their sense, which are based 'on free and thoughtful choice of intelligent human beings interacting with complex and changing environments'. They admit other methods have had limited effect, but they object to the implicit notion that 'right' values are predetermined and taught by selling, pushing or urging. Here the reader might well object to their line of argument, reasoning that other methods have had widespread effect, and that perhaps if we had been more thorough-going with these methods the effect would have been greater. It could be argued that the apparent failure of moral education is the consequence, not of method, but of too optimistic a view of human nature. Values Clarification writing could be criticized for this optimistic view that children should be free, and indeed are able, to choose, to state their interests, aspirations, beliefs and attitudes.

A *Data Diary* should help you compile a great amount of information about yourself. It is not a general diary encompassing all of your daily activities. Rather, it is a specific kind of diary. Here are some of the *Data Diary* titles from which you might select.

1. Daily Diary
How do I spend my 24 hours?

2. Confidence Diary
Keep a barometer of your varying levels of confidence and insecurity. Explain causes.

3. Decisions Diary
Life goes on, and if it is to get better for you, only you can change it. Record what decisions you made and when you took action.

4. Conflicts Diary
Describe some of the circumstances surrounding any conflicts you were involved in or may have witnessed. E.g., What were the causes? How did you react? Was it resolved? If not, could it have been resolved?

5. Current Events Diary
What is new or particularly notable in politics or business?

6. Success Diary
List days you consider successful and some things that made your day.

7. Bad Day Diary
This is a record of the events on days when it would have been better to have stayed in bed.

8. Cash Flow Diary
How did income and outflow compare today?

9. Inspiration Diary
Record deep feelings, sense of God or higher reality, spiritual or religious experience.

10. Affirmation Diary
Record nice things done for you and said about you.

11. Depression Diary
List the things and people who may have dragged you down.

12. 'I Gotta Be Me' Diary
Keep a record of where and how your actions showed your individuality.

13. Role Play Diary
Review your day in search of the times and situations when you were pretending, playing a role rather than being openly and honestly yourself.

14. Special Moments Diary
List the persons or situations that evoked affectionate feelings and thoughts because they were pleasant, intimate, and thoughtful.

15. 'Go to Hell' Diary
Some people and situations spawn anger and even hatred. Keeping a record might reveal a pattern.

16. I Learned Diary
Are you growing? This record may give you a hint.

17. Don'ts Diary
None of us likes to repeat mistakes. List people, places, food, etc., that may be 'no-nos' for you.

After you have chosen one of the *Data Diary* topics, maintain your specialized diary for at least two weeks. Then ask yourself a number of organized, serious questions and write answers in your diary. For example, in the *Disagreement Diary*, you might ask yourself these questions.

a. How many times did I firmly voice my disagreement? What was the percentage of times I did so?

b. In how many of the disagreements did I lose my temper?

c. What pattern emerges as my way of handling disagreements?

d. In observing the ways that other people handled their disagreements, do I see a pattern that I would find worthy of emulating?

From S. Simon, *Meeting Yourself Halfway*. For information about current Values Realization materials and a schedule of nationwide training workshops, contact S. Simon, Old Mountain Road, Hadley, MA 01035, USA.

I question the assumptions that other methods have proved unfruitful and that children should be free to arrive at their own values. In my experience as a teacher, parent and youth worker, children's choosing can be centred on their own interests without regard for the needs or comfort of others. It is quite possible for children—and adults, too, for that matter—to 'clarify their values' and then act in a way which causes pain to others or damage to property. The optimistic view of children takes little account of the potential for evil in human beings, and of our inability on many occasions to do what we know we ought.

Our personal values, chosen, prized and acted upon, may have ignored what intelligent people have learned down the centuries about personal relationships. Do we really want our children to make all the mistakes in behaviour, morality and relationships which we have made? I there no sense in which the values educator should help children avoid the evils of previous generations, or learn about goodness from the lives

THE SIX STAGES OF MORAL JUDGMENT

Level and Stage	Content of Stage		
	What is Right	Reasons for Doing Right	Social Perspective of Stage
Level I: Preconventional Stage 1: Heteronomous morality	Sticking to rules backed by punishment; obedience for its own sake; avoiding physical damage to persons and property.	Avoidance of punishment, superior power of authorities.	*Egocentric point of view.* Doesn't consider the interests of others or recognize that they differ from the actor's; doesn't relate two points of view. Actions considered physically rather than in terms of psychological interests of others. Confusion of authority's perspective with one's own.
Stage 2: Individualism, Instrumental purpose, and Exchange	Following rules only when in one's immediate interest; acting to meet one's own interests and needs and letting others do the same. Right is also what is fair or what is an equal exchange, deal, agreement.	To serve one's own needs or interests in a world where one has to recognize that other people also have interests.	*Concrete individualistic perspective.* Aware that everybody has interests to pursue and that these can conflict; right is relative (in the concrete individualistic sense).
Level II: Conventional Stage 3: Mutual interpersonal expectations, Relationships, and Interpersonal conformity	Living up to what is expected by people close to you or what people generally expect of a good son, brother, friend, etc. 'Being good' is important and means having good motives, showing concern for others. It also means keeping mutual relationships such as trust, loyalty, respect, and gratitude.	The need to be a good person in your own eyes and those of others; caring for others; belief in the Golden Rule; desire to maintain rules and authority that support stereotypical good behaviour.	*Perspective of the individual in relationships with other individuals.* Aware of shared feelings, agreements, and expectations which take primacy over individual interests. Relates points of view through the concrete Golden Rule, putting oneself in the other guy's shoes. Does not yet consider generalized system perspective.

of other people? Are there no principles or lessons of moral, social and personal life which the young can learn?

This really brings us to the heart of my reservations about the assumptions of Values Clarification. Few people would object to these notions of choice and freedom bound up in the democratic society we have, but it is entirely a different matter to give children the impression that all beliefs and values are equal. Do we really believe that the values of Hitler, Manson, Luther King and Mother Theresa are equally praiseworthy or good? The authors deny that Values Clarification leads to moral relativity. However, it seems to me that it is lurking about in the background. It is only one short step from saying that 'we do not believe there is one true religion, morality or political constitution' to saying that 'any purpose, motive, belief or attitude is as good as another'. The danger is that we may give the impression that 'anything goes', providing we have clarified it.

	Content of Stage		
Level and Stage	What is Right	Reasons for Doing Right	Social Perspective of Stage
Level II: Conventional (continued) Stage 4: Social system and conscience	Fulfilling duties to which you have agreed; laws to be upheld except in extreme cases where they conflict with other fixed social duties. Right is also contributing to the society, group or institution.	To keep the institution going as a whole and avoid a breakdown in the system 'if everyone did it'; imperative of conscience to meet one's defined obligations. (Easily confused with stage 3 belief in rules and authority.)	*Differentiates societal point of view from interpersonal agreement or motives.* Takes the point of view of the system that defines roles and rules; considers individual relations in terms of place in the system.
Level III: Postconventional; or principled Stage 5: Social contract or utility and individual rights	Being aware that people hold a variety of values and opinions and that most of their values and rules are relative to their group. Relative rules usually upheld in the interest of impartiality and because they are the social contract. Some nonrelative values and rights (e.g., *life* and *liberty*) must be upheld in any society and regardless of majority opinion.	A sense of obligation to law because of one's social contract to make and abide by laws for the welfare of all and for the protection of all people's rights. A feeling of contractual commitment, freely entered upon, to family, friendship, trust, and work obligations. Concern that laws and duties be based on rational calculation of overall utility, 'the greatest good for the greatest number'.	*Prior-to-society perspective.* Rational individual aware of values and rights prior to social attachments and contracts. Integrates perspectives by formal mechanisms of agreement, contract, objective impartiality, and due process. Considers moral and legal points of view; recognizes that they sometimes conflict and finds it difficult to integrate them.
Level III: Postconventional; or principled (continued) Stage 6: Universal ethical principles	Following self-chosen ethical principles. Particular laws or social agreements usually valid because they rest on such principles; when laws violate these principles, one acts in accordance with principle. Principles are universal principles of justice: equality of human rights and respect for the dignity of human beings as individuals.	The belief as a rational person in the validity of universal moral principles and a sense of personal commitment to them.	*Perspective of a moral point of view from which social arrangements derive.* Perspective is that of a rational individual recognizing the nature of morality or the fact that persons are ends in themselves and must be treated as such.

From Lawrence Kohlberg, 'Moral Stages and Moralization: The Cognitive-Developmental Approach', in *Moral Development and Behavior: Theory, Research and Social Issues,* ed. Thomas Lickona, 1976

As a Christian:

● I am not convinced that other approaches fail to the extent the authors claim.

● I find that the optimistic view of human nature takes little account of the biblical notion of sin which, in my view, makes sense of the world as we know it.

● I believe there is a danger that weighty moral issues may be trivialized. There is a lack of hierarchy in moral concepts. Moral relativism is a charge which the authors barely escape.

● I believe there is more to values and moral education than 'clarifying, choosing, prizing and acting'. It seems to me irresponsible for educators to stand by, observing their pupils rebuilding the collapsed bridges of personal, moral and social life by similar doubtful or harmful principles.

These and other points are developed further in chapter four. I would stress that my reservations concern the philosophical and belief assumptions of Values Clarification. Some of the class-room materials, the techniques, games, strategies and activities that have been generated by the work of Raths, Harmin and Simon are imaginative, ingenious and inspire me to develop my own teaching methods. They create interest, they actively involve the pupils, they tap the real feelings, attitudes, beliefs and opinions of the girls and boys. It is possible to use these strategies discriminative, along with complementary material from other approaches, even though I would reject some of the assumptions made by the authors.

There are many different approaches to PSME. I have examples of different theoretical approaches and practical class-room materials spread about the room as I type this chapter. I do not have the space to analyse many in detail, but they all appear to have ethical, philosophical or values assumptions built in.

L. Kohlberg, a leading researcher in moral development in the USA, grounds his approach in cognitive-developmental psychology, after Piaget. He proposes six stages of moral development from his research programme which are derived from levels of reasoning about hypothetical, moral dilemmas. Justice reasoning is central to moral education, particularly in his earlier work. Justice, he argues, is central to the principles underlying the Constitution and Declaration of Independence. The aim of the moral educator is to promote development by helping the pupil to reason at one stage higher in the schema than his present position. Kohlberg claims that hypothetical moral dilemmas aid this process of moral reasoning in the child. More recently he has generously admitted fallacies in his earlier work.[5] He now sees that moral education must deal with 'real' life' situations and with actions. His theory is changing and growing: 'It is a theory developing through an interchange between psychological theorists and practitioners. It started with an emphasis in psychology, led to thinking through philosophic

---

DILEMMA

In Europe, a woman is near death from a special kind of cancer. There is one drug that the doctors think might save her. It is a form of radium that a druggist in the same town has recently discovered. The drug is expensive to make, but the druggist is charging ten times what the drug cost him to make. He paid $200 for the radium and is charging $2000 for a small dose of the drug. The sick woman's husband, Heinz, goes to everyone he knows to borrow the money, but he can get together only about $1000, which is half of what it costs. He tells the druggist that his wife is dying and asks him to sell the drug cheaper or let him pay later. The druggist says, 'No, I discovered the drug and I'm going to make money from it.' Heinz is desperate and considers breaking into the man's store to steal the drug for his wife.

1. Should Heinz steal the drug? Why or why not?
2. If Heinz doesn't love his wife, should he steal the drug for her? Why or why not?
3. Suppose the person dying is not his wife but a stranger. Should Heinz steal the drug for a stranger? Why or why not?
4. (If you favor stealing the drug for a stranger): Suppose it's a pet animal he loves. Should Heinz steal to save the pet animal? Why or why not?
5. Why should people do everything they can to save another's life, anyhow?
6. It is against the law for Heinz to steal. Does that make it morally wrong? Why or why not?
7. Why should people generally do everything they can to avoid breaking the law, anyhow?
7a. How does this relate to Heinz's case?

DILEMMA

Joe is a fourteen-year-old boy who wants to go to camp very much. His father has promised him he can go if he saves up the money for it himself. Joe has worked hard at his paper route and has saved the $40 it costs to go to camp and a little more besides. But just before camp is going to start, his father changes his mind. Some of the father's friends have decided to go on a special fishing trip, and he is short of the money it would cost. He tells Joe to give him the money he has saved from the paper route. Joe doesn't want to give up going to camp, so he thinks of refusing to give his father the money.

1. Should Joe refuse to give his father the money? Why or why not?
2. In what way is the fact that Joe earned the money himself something very important for the father to consider?
3. The father promised Joe he could go to camp if he earned the money. Is that promise something very important for the father or Joe to consider? Why or why not?
4. Why in general should a promise be kept?
5. Is it important to keep a promise to someone you don't know well and probably won't see again? Why or why not?
6. What do you think is the most important thing for a good son to be concerned about in his relationship with his father in this or other situations?
6a. Why is that important?
7. What do you think is the most important thing for a good father to be concerned about in his relationship with his son in this or other situations?
7a. Why is that important?

From R. H. Hersh, D. P. Paolitto, J. Reimer, *Promoting Moral Growth*, 1979

ssues, and proceeded to expansion nd revision in the light of ontinuing experience in class-rooms nd community meetings in a "just-community" school.'

Any summary of such an immense mount of research and writing is ound to be inadequate. I ecommend interested readers to efer to Hersh for a very lucid ccount, and for applications of the heory in the class-room.

Readers may well have reservations r objections to the possible aturalistic fallacy of deriving an ought' from an 'is' (saying what hould be from what already exists) n Kohlberg's work, or to the levation of moral reasoning to the ighest place in the 'moral life'. eaders may be critical of Kohlberg's research methods, or of is six stages of moral development. t may be worth examining the stages nd enquiring whether our own nderstanding of ethics matches with Kohlberg's categories.

Kohlberg and his associates found ertain stages of moral reasoning in eople in the USA, UK and in other arts of the world. They build their pproach on trying to encourage hildren to reason about moral ilemmas at one stage higher, thus romoting what they believe is moral evelopment.

In the UK the Farmington Trust, argely through the work of John Wilson,[6] have also majored on moral easoning as the basis for moral ducation. This approach has grown ut of philosophy rather than sychology. Skills in moral thinking re the priority, rather than mparting specific values. Wilson vants to acquaint children with norality as a subject or area of hought, and make them aware of the echniques, skills and qualities equired to get answers to moral uestions. He believes he has the ight methods for rational creatures o solve their moral problems. He ells us[7] that for fifteen years he has een trying to persuade educators hat there is a set of attributes emanded by pure reason.

Quoted here is Wilson's full list of Moral Components which he argues re required by logic to designate vhat it means to be educated in

morality.[8]

Wilson's critics might suggest that his approach is rather like a GCE 'O' level examination in moral philosophy. However, this is rather unfair. The methodology does offer a way of teaching moral reasoning and studying topics such as 'Cruise missiles', 'euthanasia', 'How do I know what is right in a given circumstance?'—in fact any issue or

topic of an ethical nature. My greatest reservation about approaches to PSME that emphasize moral reasoning is that they fail to address the central question of morality—the fundamental moral problem of knowing what is good, knowing what we should do, but not being able to do it. It is crystallized in this classic statement by St Paul: 'For what I do is not the good I want to do; no, the

FULL LIST OF MORAL COMPONENTS

PHIL(HC)	Having the concept of a 'person'.
PHILL(CC)	Claiming to use this concept in an overriding, prescriptive, universalised (O,P and U) principle.
PHIL(RSF) (DO & PO)	Having feelings which support this principle, either of a 'duty-oriented' (DO) or a 'person-oriented' (PO) kind.
EMP(HC)	Having the concepts of various emotions (Moods, etc.).
EMP(1)(Cs)	Being able, in practice, to identify emotions, etc., in oneself, when these are at a conscious level.
EMP(1)(Ucs)	Ditto, when the emotions are at an unconscious level.
EMP(2)(Cs)	Ditto, in other people, when at a conscious level.
EMP(2)(Ucs)	Ditto, when at an unconscious level.
GIG(1)(KF)	Knowing other ('hard') facts relevant to moral decisions.
GIG(1)(KS)	Knowing sources of facts (where to find out) as above.
GIG(2)(VC)	'Knowing how': a 'skill' element in dealing with moral situations, as evinced in verbal communication with others.
GIG(2)(NVC)	Ditto, in non-verbal communication.
KRAT(1)(RA)	Being, in practice, 'relevantly alert' to (noticing) moral situations, and seeing them as such (describing them in terms of PHIL, etc. above).
KRAT(1)(TT)	Thinking thoroughly about such situations, and bringing to bear whatever PHIL, EMP, and GIG one has.
KRAT(1)(OUP)	As a result of the foregoing, making an overriding, prescriptive and universalised decision to act in others' interests.
KRAT(2)	Being sufficiently whole-hearted, free from unconscious counter-motivation, etc. to carry out (when able) the above decision in practice.

These 'components' ('constituents', 'necessary features', 'pieces of equipment', or whatever it's best to call them) are of course **logical** and not **empirical**. I mean that they are simply an expansion of what it **means to be** 'educated in morality', what characteristics are required by logic. They are not mental forces or entities of any kind. They represent the (only proper) objectives for any attempt at moral education, independent of class or culture or any other empirical feature. In similar ways, presumably a

(logical) list of attributes forming what we mean by 'a good scientist' or 'a well-educated historian' could be produced (though I am not aware of any very satisfactory lists of this sort) — and would need to be, if we were to be really clear about the objectives of teaching science or history.

Reproduced from J. Wilson, 'First Steps in Moral Education' in *The Ethical Dimensions of the School Curriculum*, ed. L. O. Ward

evil I do not want to do—this I keep on doing.' I may be able to reason my way to knowing how to think and act morally, but what can strengthen my resolve and motivate my will to do it? Further, the reduction of morality to reasoning may leave out the imagination, emotions, faith commitment, the inculcation of habits, and socialization—all of which may contribute to a person's morality.

A programme of PSME to which I have referred several times and which is concerned with wider aspects of morality and personal and social education is *Lifeline*. The project worked from the belief that our principal adult responsibility is to 'help boys and girls live well'. The notions of 'caring and choosing', and 'a considerate lifestyle', are assumptions built into the project. The emotional dimension to interpersonal problems is highlighted: 'but being more intelligent does not necessarily mean that you are better able to find and apply solutions to interpersonal problems, where the key is so often emotional.'[9]

Lifeline built its teaching materials on 'significant situations technique', that is, the empirical investigation of what boys and girls said is 'good' and

---

1. How far can a friend reasonably expect your support? If you believe there are limits state them.

2. If you have ever been put in a difficult position by a friend expecting your support, describe exactly what happened—without using any names of course.

3. Collect examples from other members of your group or class of situations in which an individual was not expected to let a friend down.

Reproduced from P. McPhail, *And how are we feeling today?* Cambridge University Press, 1977

'bad', and how they learned their behaviour. McPhail and his associates researched extensively to anchor moral and social education in the actual experience of boys and girls. I think that among the factors explaining the popularity of *Lifeline*, must be the favourable reactions of the pupils. Adolescent children actually identified with the material—it was about them. The project also provided practical materials which teachers could use. It was ready-made. In addition, it fitted in with what schools wanted of their pupils, 'a theory of morals in which concern for another's needs, interests and feelings as well as one's own is cheered and lack of consideration is booed'.[10]

The programme has three parts: 'In Other People's Shoes'; 'Proving the Rule'; and 'What Would You Have Done?' The first part provides a series of cards depicting situations designed to help children become sensitive to others, to learn to think about the consequences of their actions, and to help them consider other people's points of view. The second is a series of booklets, depicting situations, relationships and conflicts where pupils are invited to explore their own and other people's interests, the merits and demerits of various points of view, so that they can find out what beliefs and values they wish to hold. The third part is a series of booklets dealing with historical situations designed to expand the universe of

---

the pupil, the understanding of moral problems in a wider context.

Much of this original material from the 60s and 70s can still be used with great effect, even though there have been changes in the attitudes of young people and in their culture. McPhail writes about these in his current work. There is no doubt that much can be learned from the work of McPhail and his associates. He roots or, to use his word, 'anchors' PSME in the pupil's world. He is not talking about abstract principles but about young people's problems, decisions, relationships, and situations which directly affect them. *Lifeline* also provided a pattern for projects which were to follow, such as *Startline 8–1* Moral Education Project, and later the Health Education Council Project 12–18, *Living Well*[11]. Readers who are unfamiliar with these projects might look at the handbooks. They contain much that can be learned about PSME and are full of practical ideas about the 'how to' in class-rooms. There is a wealth of guidance about actual class-room methods: discussion, role play, use of stimulus material such as photographs, drama, and imaginative writing. The philosophy adopted is also spelt out to the reader.

You are given what is generally regarded as a fair punishment for deliberately breaking a school rule.

What do you do?

Reproduced from *Lifeline*, Schools Council Project in Moral Education, Longman, 1972

A friend doesn't let you down – ever.

Reproduced from *Living Well*, Health Education Council Project 12–18

It is the philosophy underlying the McPhail work (a philosophy popular with teachers because it is pragmatic, appearing to rest on the facts) that philosophers such as R. Straughan are concerned about. Straughan argues that 'considerateness' cannot be set up as the sole principle of PSME, and that to derive the principle of considerateness from the so-called set of facts on which the programme is based is logically very shaky. The fact that surveys of English children show that they happen to use 'good' and 'bad' in these ways cannot establish that morality is therefore necessarily about considerateness. McPhail appears to fall willingly into the naturalistic fallacy, deriving values from facts, the 'ought' from the 'is'.

Further, McPhail maintains that a considerate style of life results in happiness and health for the individual because it earns acceptance and supportive feedback. Not only do others benefit, but the individuals themselves gain: 'They are generally treated better by other people; they enjoy life, are healthy and develop identity and personality which enables them to cope, even when their considerate behaviour does not earn considerate treatment in return.'[12]

Straughan criticizes this values position which he describes as attempts to establish moral rules and principles by appealing to the notion of human welfare in various forms'. Straughan's lucid and non-technical book, *Can We Teach Children To Be Good?*[13] is a very helpful introduction to elucidating philosophical assumptions in approaches to PSME. I recommend it to readers who may be interested in moral philosophy. Kathleen Gow's excellent book, *Yes, Virginia, There is Right and Wrong*,[14] makes a careful scrutiny of assumptions and underlying values in Values Education in Canadian schools.

I have looked at Values Clarification, Kohlberg's Moral Development, Wilson's moral reasoning and McPhail's Moral Education Project to illustrate the central thesis of this chapter that PSME does have value assumptions or philosophical orientations underlying both theory and practice. I have tried to uncover the foundations of these approaches and to suggest ways in which they might be questioned or considered 'suspect'. I have found much to admire, emulate, learn from and relate to my own class-room in all these approaches to the more 'moral' and 'personal' aspects of PSME, although I do have considerable misgiving and doubts, and in some cases reject the philosophical ground of these approaches.

The existentialism, naturalism and humanism which underlie them, the psychological and philosophical perspectives adopted, leave me dissatisfied and with many reservations, both as a teacher and as a Christian.

What then do I have to offer? What alternatives can be suggested? What philosophical or value assumptions may a teacher base his work upon? The PSME of our pupils is vital, as I argued in previous chapters. How then should we proceed in our schools? This is where I believe the Christian faith has a distinctive contribution to make.

Footnotes

1. R. S. Peters, *Ethics and Education*, p.91.
2. D. Bridges, P. Scrimshaw, *Values and Authority in Schools*, p.2.
3. S. Simon, *Meeting Yourself Halfway*.
4. L. Raths, M. Harmin, S. Simon, *Values and Teaching*.
5. See Foreword to R. H. Hersh, D. P. Paolitto, J. Reimer, *Promoting Moral Growth*.
6. See J. Wilson, *A Teacher's Guide to Moral Education*.
7. 'First Steps in Moral Education' in L. O. Ward's, *The Ethical Dimensions of the School Curriculum*, p.127.
8. See also *Practical Methods of Moral Education*.
9. P. McPhail, J. R. Ungoed-Thomas, H. Chapman, *Moral Education in the Secondary School*, p.5.
10. *Op. cit*, p.49.
11. P. McPhail, C. Rainbow, M. Rogers, *Living Well*.
12. P. McPhail, *op. cit.*, p.3.
13. George Allen and Unwin, 1982.
14. Wiley, 1980.

CHAPTER 4

A DISTINCTIVE CHRISTIAN CONTRIBUTION?

The Christian faith and ethic, and the Christian teacher, can have an important role in the Personal, Social and Moral Education of children. Of course, I am not suggesting that Christians alone have a legitimate interest in this field of education. I have friends and colleagues who do not share my faith, but who work hard for this aspect of children's development. Humanists, Muslims, Marxists—many colleagues not professing a particular label—all share the concern of Christians for the moral, social, personal, and political welfare of young people. Even so, I would claim that Christians can in fact make a distinctive and unique contribution to children's education.

But first let me define my terms. The word 'Christian' has no commonly agreed definition. It can mean, 'one who lives a virtuous life', or 'one who attends a church regularly'. It is often applied loosely to anyone who has been baptised or christened. In this chapter I use the term more precisely, going back to source. In the New Testament, Christians were followers of 'the Way', they were followers or disciples of the Jesus Way. A Christian in the sense I wish to use the term is a person who accepts the claims of Christ in the Gospels, and who submits him- or herself to the rule of living the 'Jesus Way' as described and expanded in the New Testament.

In this sense, then, a Christian is not one born into a Christian country but, to use St John's phrase, one born again into the kingdom of God. A Christian is a person who has encountered God through faith in Jesus Christ. Some people feel overwhelmed by God's love, others awed by his majesty, some convicted of their moral weakness or their sin

in the presence of the holiness of God. Some people describe the experience as being irresistibly drawn to the character or the passion of Jesus. Christians, as in any special subject, have their own language for these experiences. They talk of repentance, faith, atonement, forgiveness, and the life of the Spirit. Christianity, then, is not a set of ancient dogmas, but a living

---

'The Spirit of the Lord is on me, because he has anointed me to preach good news to the poor. He has sent me to proclaim freedom for the prisoners and recovery of sight to the blind, to release the oppressed, to proclaim the year of the Lord's favour.' Jesus, quoted in Luke 4:18-19

---

relationship with God, active fellowship with Jesus of Nazareth.

This understanding is important, because it is central to the development of my argument.

First I want to consider the 'important role' Christians can have in their school. Educational documents and writers are recognizing the place of moral, spiritual, social and political dimensions to the curriculum. Surely Christians should not remain silent, or fettered by some modern mythological concept of neutrality in the class-room. Christians have insights into these dimensions. They have collections of sacred writings, examples of persons living exemplary lives, which they should contribute alongside other evidence and traditions. Christians have a legitimate right to see that the genuine light which Christianity throws on moral, social or personal issues is considered by boys and girls.

This is not indoctrination. I am not interested in indoctrinating my pupils. I want young people in state schools to consider a variety of views and insights into personal, social and moral problems. I do not wish to make children adopt a particular attitude to life, indeed I cannot do that. But I do want them to have the chance of considering and discussing a Christian understanding of life issues.

● The first contribution Christians should make—and make boldly—is to ensure that, alongside other opinions and views, Christianity has a fair hearing. It seems popular in some publications to scour the world for insights into human problems while missing key Christian understanding that have deeply influenced our own culture.

● The second significant contribution that Christians should be making to this area of education is to live the life they profess, to *put into practice what they say they believe*. Faith, in the Christian sense, is not just an intellectual assent to a set of beliefs, but personal commitment to the Christian Way. Humility in making truth claims, a spirit of repentance for our weaknesses and a genuine love for people, will help validate our claims to understand truth. If Christians are seen to live the life they profess—if they demonstrate the 'life abundant' Christian joy, and manifest Christ's victory over sin, through 'walking in the Spirit' as St Paul puts it, then they can have a powerful impact on children. It is essential to practise what we preach.

It is important that the teacher's thinking and planning takes account of ethnic minority cultures.

Douglas Hamblin and Ken David have recently called for a review of the provision which schools are making for the pastoral care of their pupils. Christians who are living in the 'life and power of the Spirit of Christ' have an outstanding contribution to make. We are called to express to our pupils the self-giving *agape* love that Christ had for people. He graciously accepted 'publicans and sinners'; he was moved with compassion for suffering; he gave up his life in sacrificial love for others.

Christian teachers are called to work out in concrete terms what this *agape* love means in their relationships with pupils. Christian love goes beyond 'respect for persons' or what *loco parentis* may reasonably demand. *Agape* seeks the pupils' welfare, their ultimate good, even when it costs. The pupil's disobedience, or demanding behaviour may threaten our personal convenience or comfort. It may call for a second 'long mile' of patience, but this is the distinctive contribution of Christ to pastoral care.

It is well known that children are far more impressed by what we are, than by what we say. Are we ready to listen to stories about quarrels that we may find irritating? Are we concerned for Sylvia when she has lost her anorak for the third time in a term? Are we prepared to take children out camping, hostelling, on visits? Are we open to listen to children and appreciate them—not only when they are pleasant and responsive, but when they are awkward and disruptive, or when we feel tired or 'end-of-termish'? These are the extra contributions that Christian teachers should be making.

We all fall short of these ideals, of course. We need to translate our beliefs into action, to appropriate the grace, love and power of God which is available to us. We can also pray for our work as a class or form teacher. We can show the pastoral care of Jesus. Of course, we all make mistakes, we fail, we feel defeated: but the heart of the Christian message is that help is available. Jesus Christ will pick us up again, again and again. His work continues through us.

These last paragraphs may appear rather theological to readers who do not themselves hold a Christian faith. So let me refer to the series of books called *Active Tutorial Work*[1] to illustrate how teachers with a wide range of beliefs are contributing to the pastoral care and personal, social and moral development of their pupils. Lancashire Education Authority, which leads the field in many ways, has jointly published this series, which is a programme of developmental group work. Running through the books there are threads of children's self-awareness, learning and study skills, social skills and coping skills, personal relationships, critical incidents in growing up through school life, and friendships. Here are rich sources of ideas, topics, class-room methods, and actual class-room materials. They are a 'must' for any teacher in the pastoral or Personal, Social and Moral Education field.

Many teachers have welcomed the publication of these programmes, and I thoroughly recommend them to Christian teachers as a source of ideas. As in the wider pastoral and guidance fields, I believe Christians have important qualities and skills which they can put to good effect in form periods, tutorial groups, and pastoral education programmes of work. A capacity to reflect about human behaviour, relationships, and right and wrong, an ability to put ourselves in another person's shoes, and concern about the problems and evils in society are Christian qualities (although not exclusively so). They can be helpful attributes in this kind of work. Christians should be eager to review and improve the methods of teaching they adopt. Active Tutorial Work demands imagination, different kinds of teacher-pupil relationships, and the flexible use of class-room space by the teacher. The emphasis is not so much on instruction in content, but on processes in groups, particularly discussion.

Another approach to Personal, Social and Moral Education is through Health Education. The Health Education 13–18 Project is not just concerned with hygiene and preventive aspects of health. The days of 'drugs, nits and sex talks' are over! The World Health Organization defines health as 'a state of complete physical, mental and social well-being, not merely the absence of disease or infirmity'. The project's Introductory Handbook explains that by health they mean the power to live a full, adult, living, breathing life in close contact with what we love. Health is the desire to be all that we are capable of becoming.

The aims of the project sound familiar. They are similar to the more moral and values dimensions of Pring's matrix. Their aims are not only to give basic health knowledge and understanding of human development, and to help young people to adapt to change in themselves and their environment, but also to help them explore and understand feelings, attitudes and values in themselves and others. The theme of 'choice', which determines future health and life-style, also recurs. Eight areas of health are identified:

- personal health and body management
- parenthood
- relationships
- growth and development
- community health
- food selection
- safety and first-aid
- the environment

Advice on curriculum planning, co-ordinating a programme, practical class-room materials, worksheets, games and activities are included in the pack. This is one of the best packages of Personal, Social and Moral Education it is possible to buy. Much of what experienced teachers have developed over years is distilled and shared in the package.

How, then, does this project relate to the central contention of this chapter that Christians have a distinctive contribution to make?
- In the first place, one of the principal notions in the project is the wider use of 'health'. Health is related to wholeness and well-being. No doubt the humanistic educators and the human potential movement in psychology in the USA have had some influence on this notion of health. Christians have a vital part to

Development as a PERSON	FACTUAL KNOWLEDGE	UNDERSTANDING & RELEVANT CONCEPTS	ATTITUDE & DISPOSITION	PRACTICAL APPLICATION HABITS & SKILLS
BEING A PERSON				
SOCIAL RELATIONS				
MORAL PERSPECTIVE				
Development as a PERSON OF A CERTAIN KIND or SORT				
MORAL VALUES & DISPOSITIONS				
IDEALS — Religion — Life-style				
POLITICAL PERSPECTIVE — race — sexism — environment issues				
SOCIAL FUNCTION — Life-style — Career choice				
HEALTH — Physical — Mental				

Reproduced from R. Pring, 'Personal and Social Development:
Some principles for Curriculum Planning', *Cambridge Journal of Education*, Vol. 12, No. 1, 1982

...ay here because they should clearly [b]e concerned with the wholeness and [w]ell-being of their pupils.

Second, the concept of wholeness [and] well-being is foundational to [C]hristian doctrine and life. The [H]ebrew word *shalom* is related to [pe]ace and well-being. The key [C]hristian concept of salvation has [H]ebrew roots of breadth, ease and [sa]fety, and Greek roots of cure, [re]covery, remedy, welfare, as well as the more familiar idea of 'rescue'. Salvation is the 'action or result of deliverance or preservation from danger or disease, implying safety, health and prosperity', as one theologian puts it. In the New Testament, salvation is deliverance from the captivity of sin, its penalty and power in our lives. As Paul puts it, 'in Christ' we are delivered from the kingdom of darkness, through what Christians call the atonement.

The 'good news' that Jesus preached, taught and brought to people was deliverance and salvation. Paul declares that he was not ashamed of this 'good news' because it is the 'power of God for the salvation of everyone who believes'. He was not embarrassed by it, indeed he gloried in the cross of Christ, since through his death we are set free. He saw multitudes released from impoverished lives dominated by self and evil into this salvation, this well-being, a growing wholeness and fulfillment.

Some people appear to be suspicious of this radical concept of health, this Christian doctrine of salvation, this invitation by God to newness of life. Many of the projects I have reviewed have much to recommend, but they are not radical enough. They are excellent as far as they go, but they miss out the spiritual dimension which is most important of all. Mankind's relationship with his Maker is the vital basis for Personal, Social and Moral Education.

I am aware that for many this will be the most contentious sentence in this book, but none the less I believe it to be the most important idea I have to contribute to any discussion about this area. This is a distinctive contribution that Christian teachers must make to the personal, social and moral development of their pupils. This is not to deny the tremendous amount of first-class work teachers are doing in developing pupils' self-esteem, fostering sensitivity to the

What Christianity Supplies

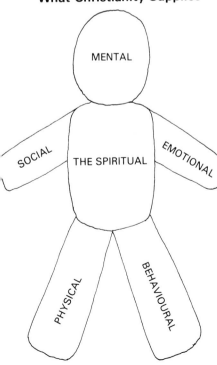

C. S. Lewis, 'Men Without Chests'.

beliefs of others and equipping children with decision-making techniques. Health Education 13–18 is evidence of this admirable work. What Christians have to offer is an extra dimension: the notion of Christian salvation-wholeness.

I want to urge Christian readers to relate their faith directly to their occupations in education. I am not advocating evangelism in a state school. It is not my job, or that of any other teacher, to preach Christianity to a captive audience. However, we may share Christian insights and perspectives alongside other views. Christians may present their understanding of the self-giving love which is crucial to Christian marriage when pupils are following courses on preparation for parenthood. We may argue the case for honesty, justice, tolerance, chastity, forgiveness or any other Christian virtue in lessons about moral questions. None of the various approaches and packages of curriculum materials is value free. Any teacher can smuggle in ideas of 'the good', presuppositions about the 'nature of man', 'the good life', 'what children should be' simply by the topics chosen, the materials used, and the methods adopted. Humanistic values, relativistic thinking, and pluralistic notions appear to be implicit in some of the approaches we have looked at.

If we present the evidence of a variety of opinions on controversial issues, argue our own Christian beliefs but allow our pupils their proper right to think for themselves in a state school in a democratic society, we are being thoroughly professional. Cries of 'indoctrination' can be dismissed. It would not be ethical to present only our own view, or to try to persuade children against their will, particularly in a school like my own, which has broad humanistic egalitarian principles with a pluralistic climate of values. There is tolerance in the school's philosophy for a variety of faiths in the multi-cultural society which is Luton. We need to be thoroughly professional; we need also to be thoroughly Christian.

I have argued that Christian teachers have insights which should

legitimately be considered alongside other views on social, personal, moral or political issues. I have suggested that Christian teachers can have a special contribution to a school's pastoral care by their practice of Christ's love. They have attributes and skills which may enrich tutorial work or pastoral education. Further, I have reasoned that Christians have a distinctive dimension to bring to Personal, Social and Moral Education which derives from the doctrine and experience of Christian salvation-wholeness—and they should share this with their pupils. I now want to consider the unique contribution of Christianity itself.

This uniqueness is concerned with the truth claims of Christianity. There is an exclusiveness about the claims of Jesus of Nazareth which seems arrogant to many minds influenced by relativism and pluralism in the realm of beliefs and values. If we were concerned only with matters of opinion, of personal preference, then Values Clarification or the neutral chairmanship approaches would be ideal in our schools. However, I believe we are concerned with what is right, and with what is true, rather than with opinions or preferences.

In the space I have available I can offer only a few ideas to stimulate further thinking and reading. I believe Christianity provides an integrated philosophy of life which should undergird a school's ideals and practices. All schools have both explicit and open, and implicit and hidden, philosophical beliefs. Often there are conflicting assumptions and practices within the same school. Kohlberg and his associates have organized schools with 'just communities'. Other leading thinkers have proposed 'respect for persons', or principles of ethics derived from pure reason as the grounding for school life. I believe we need Christians who will not only work as individuals in schools, but who will set up schools with a Christian rather than humanistic philosophy. Why?

● First of all, there needs to be a match between a school's ethical and social principles, and its practice for the sake of an effective personal, ocial and moral education. I believe that the Christian community can do his effectively.

• Second, Christians have both the laims for truth and the power to ccomplish what is needed. These re not mindless assertions. Christian thics are based not on the autonomy f reason, 'the greatest good for the reatest number' or on 'self-interest', ut on the notion of revelation. rinciples of human conduct, elationships and knowledge of right nd wrong are derived from the elief that there is a supreme being vho has made known his divine will bout these principles through evelation. This is not an ethical cop-ut, with appeals to authority to scape the pain of decision. It is ational submission to a superior ind. I am out-reasoned when I read ne Bible. To put it another way, it, entirely reasonable to me that a esigner should best know the right perating principles for his vention.

A key notion for the Christian is aith'. The validity of the truth aims Christianity makes cannot be nally argued, established by logic one. The Christian presuppositions out the existence of God, about hat the Bible says about rgiveness, repentance, love, or out principles for life are not just teoretical hypotheses. As Colin rown puts it: 'Their validity is sted by whatever is built upon em. If they are incapable of bearing eight they must be scrapped and hers sought.'[2] The Christian approaches ersonal, Social and Moral ducation through his reason and notion, but confronted with the ivine' adopts faith in his adequacy. As Paul expresses it in Corinthians 3: 'The wisdom of this orld is foolishness in God's sight.' he validity of what is understood r faith is confirmed in experience. he Christian has a lot to say about e mind. After all, Jesus, according St John, is the *Logos*—the Word. ne Christian finds his faith ninently rational. His reason helps m understand the principles for life nich God has revealed. St Paul eaks about the hollowness of man philosophy, the futility of

thinking and deceptiveness of knowledge when we leave God out of account. He talks about the 'renewed mind' that we may prove what 'God's will is—his good, pleasing and perfect will'. Christians do not reject reason, but they derive their unique understanding of the 'good' and the 'perfect' in personal, social and moral matters from revelation and faith. The writings of Francis Schaeffer[3] may appeal to readers who are interested in the truth claims of Christianity. Colin Chapman's *The Case for Christianity* and David Matthew's article 'It's All in the Mind—or is it?—The Stronghold of Intellectualism' are also helpful.[4]

Christian ethics proceed from our understanding of the nature of God. We should derive principles for Personal, Social and Moral Education from what we know about God through the Christian scriptures, through the life and teaching of Jesus. Christian teachers may find their training and the intellectual climate of their school working actively against the principles of the kingdom of God. For many years I worked in schools with underlying clarification principles which were not in harmony with my Christian faith. As St Paul reminds us powerfully, 'though we walk in the flesh (i.e. live according to the fallen world) we do not fight as the world does, for the weapons we fight with are not the weapons of this world, but on the contrary they have divine power to demolish strongholds. We pull down every argument and pretension that sets itself up against the knowledge of God, and we *take every thought captive and make it obey Christ*'.

Godliness, righteousness, justice, law, self-giving love are Christian principles which are touchstones for the organization of school communities. Truthfulness, respect for evidence, the value of persons, and forgiveness and repentance in human relationships in school are principles which should infuse school life, not because our reason demands it, or because of their value in terms of human welfare, but because God demands it, because they are necessarily derived from who God is. There appears at first glance to be

much common ground between the secular humanist and the biblical Christian. But the two diverge on the fundamental notions of the nature of God and the nature of man. I believe that principles for organizing a school should take account of a Christian understanding of human sin and of the nature of evil. Moral autonomy, so highly prized by many thinkers, is the very activity which shuts us out from the life of God. When we choose our own way rather than God's way, we separate ourselves from the benefits of the kingdom of God. Sin involves rebellion, turning away from God, disobeying the known will of God, and falling short of his standards. It is this principle of pride and selfishness, and opposition to God which operates in every human being. A school needs to take account of this unrighteousness, this disposition to evil which infects the personalities of both staff and pupils. I find that teachers are increasingly aware of this in many children in their classes. We are so used to the naturalistic explanations supplied by sociology and psychology for every deviation that we fail to recognize the principle of sin at work within the child, and within the teacher too.

The biblical view of people is that they are of immense worth, capable of noble acts and creative genius. They have the marks of the Creator upon them. On the other hand, the principle of sin stains our character, our mind, our attitudes and behaviour. Without the Christian doctrine and experience of redemption, school-children remain under the influence of sin and evil, or as the Bible puts it: 'in the dominion of darkness, under Satan's power'. We have power to accomplish what is needed. Human sin, the power of evil over boys and girls, needs to be defeated—and the power is available. Liberation into forgiveness, self-acceptance and self-esteem, meaning and purpose in life, worshipping, serving God and the community, is available in the Christian faith. Young people need an integrated view of life, not just a personal search for some meaning, but a search for the truth. As Francis Schaeffer argues, Christians have the opportunity to speak clearly of the fact that the Christian faith has the very thing that modern man has despaired of—a world-view which takes account of the whole of life. Christians should not let their own imperfect understanding or practice of the faith silence their witness to the gospel: for it truly is the 'good news' which boys and girls, men and women so desperately need.

Let Christian teachers speak up, put their faith into practice, and boldly relate their faith to their work. We need the Christian faith expressed in schools so that the spiritual dimension of personal, social and moral development can be fully expressed and practised. I am fully aware of the questions, problems and dilemmas which flow from what I have been saying.

● Ideally, should all schools be Christian? Yes, I believe so, because the Christian way is the one that works in practice, and it claims to be true.

● Can Christians work in schools where there is a non-Christian philosophy? Yes. They are needed to ensure that Christian insights have consideration alongside other views. Christian teachers have a distinctive contribution to make.

● On what grounds can Christians argue for a Christian philosophy for schools where we have a multi-cultural and pluralistic society? All schools have a belief or value system. They should come out in the open about their values. Christianity claims to be the truth and it provides what young people—and indeed society—needs.

● In practice how could Christian schools be set up? This is not the place to develop the case for Christian schools. I believe Christians should work within the state system where possible, and within the church community privately.

● In a state school with a Christian philosophy how do you avoid charges of indoctrination? Indoctrination takes places where one exclusive view is imposed on children without regard for their intelligent decision. A Christian philosophy must allow other viewpoints to be made fairly, and to be considered and assessed by pupils. Christians cannot force people to become Christian: that is the antithesis of the gospel. The life of the kingdom of God would be expressed through the life of the school in the same way that non-Christian values and ideals are expressed and fostered in schools—through the organization, rituals, relationships between people,

discipline, and in the subjects taught.

I would not want in any way to deny or undervalue the excellent work being done in schools by teachers who do not share my own Christian faith. I meet teachers at conferences around the country who inspire me with their devotion and enthusiasm. Their creative ideas fire the imagination and put many Christian teachers to shame. Christians and non-Christians alike have put together a range of teaching materials which provide first-class ideas and practical suggestions for the class-room. Even so, when all is said and due praise given, there is still an important role for Christian teachers to play. There is a distinctive and unique contribution that Christians may make to the personal, social and moral development of their pupils.

Footnotes

1. J. Baldwin, H. Wells, *Active Tutorial Work*.
2. C. Brown, *Philosophy and the Christian Faith*.
3. F. Schaeffer, *The God Who is There*; *Escape from Reason*; *Death in the City*.
4. In *Restoration*.

PART 2

AIMS AND METHODS

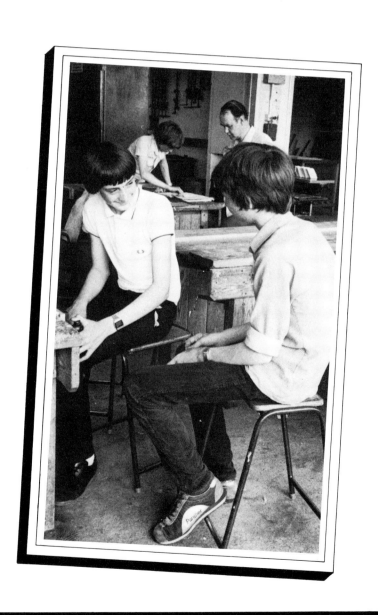

CHAPTER 5

PLANNING PRINCIPLES
AND AIMS

Part One surveyed the scene of Personal, Social and Moral Education. In this second part, I want to invite the reader to consider practical principles and issues in planning and organizing this work in schools, and methods and materials for class-room use.

Many teachers I have met at conferences around the country have become involved in this area of the curriculum without having worked out their planning principles. Teachers are essentially practically minded. When faced with a class of children I want to know what I am going to do, and what the children will be required to do. Knowing your subject, being confident of the way you teach, and being prepared with something for the pupils to do are essential, both for effective learning and for the teacher's own peace of mind.

When I examine syllabuses or schemes of work prepared by colleagues I find they are concerned mainly with lists of content, descriptions of areas of knowledge to be covered. Examination syllabuses are often similar: the content is laid out, but there is less attention to teaching method, and only infrequent reference to planning principles (for example, aims, specific objectives, or content analysed into concepts, skills, as well as factual knowledge). All this suggests that teachers may be less familiar with working out their planning principles than with making lists of content. Yet I want to suggest that the planning principles are vital for a clear understanding of what we teachers are doing and what we expect our pupils to learn in a notoriously vague area of the curriculum.

Lawrence Stenhouse has surveyed the debate about aims and behavioural objectives, versus processes and principles of procedure in planning for the class-room in chapters 5, 6 and 7 of *An Introduction to Curriculum Research and Development*.[1] These chapters give the reader a very clear understanding of the issues involved. My own concern lies in the fact that teachers get started in pastoral education, or in the social, moral or political dimensions of the curriculum, without even thinking about their aims. Form tutors come on courses because they have been asked to work with Active Tutorial Work Books, without having had time to reflect about what they are doing and why. Schools must surely have a purpose. Our Personal, Social and Moral Education should have intentions or aims.

Back in 1949, Ralph Tyler[2] was suggesting that broad aims should be broken down into behavioural objectives. He argued that teachers should state what kind of behaviour is to be developed and the content or area of life in which this behaviour is to operate. The intended learning outcomes should be specific, clear and precise according to this view of planning. Hilda Taba draws the distinction between aims as broad statements of intention, and objectives as detailed specific outcomes desired. Benjamin Bloom and others have developed a taxonomy of educational objectives which will be familiar to generations of student teachers.

Writers such as Stenhouse, R.S. Peters and E.W. Eisner have drawn attention to the limitations of seeing education as a means to an end, external from the process of education itself. Where information or skills are being taught, pre-specified objectives are helpful, especially when we come to assess what has been learned. Where we

centre on knowledge, understanding or criteria, on the deep structure of disciplines such as Literature, Religion, Music, Art or Science we do not have specific behavioural outcomes in mind, but a deepening of understanding. They argue that procedures, concepts and criteria cannot be adequately translated into performance levels, without distortion of knowledge and trivialization. Stenhouse's *Humanitie. Curriculum Project* and Bruner's *Man: A Course of Study* are examples of curriculum materials built on procedural principles, or the process model of planning.

Where does all this leave the teacher of Personal, Social and Moral Education? In a Schools Council publication, *Personal and Social Education in Secondary Schools*,[3] which came into my hands recently, the working party state that 'they involved themselves in searching debate as to whether the behavioural outcomes (or product), or the procedures of operation (or process) should be emphasized'. It is this debate which I invite the reader to join. What kind of aims should we have? Surely we ought to know what we are doing, and why, in the class-room? Without aims we merely blunder about. Our teaching method selection of content, and choice of learning tasks can flow from the decisions we make about our aims.

I believe there are areas of our work where both kinds of aims— behavioural objectives *and* process or procedural principles—apply. There are facts, simple information we may wish our pupils to know: about the police, law, different types of jobs, what kind of beliefs Marxists, Muslims or Hindus have about death, about health and sex education, and so on. This information may be essential in itsel or it may be important as a basis for other activities (such as choices, sensitivity training, formation of attitudes, opinions, beliefs). We might state our behavioural objective in these terms:

● 'We wish our pupils to be able to state clearly to a visiting Inspector three diseases which are linked with the smoking of cigarettes.'

or:

● 'We wish our pupils to be able to explain in their end-of-term test the three reasons why we have laws in this country.'

We have pre-specified our intended learning outcomes clearly, precisely and specifically. We have stated the conditions under which the behaviour may be tested or observed.

Behavioural objectives may also be stated about skills we wish the children to learn. These may be communication skills, social skills, or moral decision skills. Consider these examples:

● We wish our group of eight, less-able 12-year-olds to be able to answer the telephone with confidence and take a message accurately, after a series of lessons and practice. These skills will be tested using the school telephone.

● We wish the head girl to meet our visitor at the school gate, take him to the prefects' common-room, and there introduce him to the sixth-form prefects, before his talk on 'The Freedom of the Press' in the lecture theatre. Later, in tutorial time, discussion will take place on 'meeting and introducing people'.

In both cases I have tried to state clearly and precisely the intended outcomes, and I have indicated the conditions under which they will be tested or observed. The more complex the skills, particularly where there are several linked together (as in these cases), the more difficult it is to state specific objectives.

When we look again at Pring's matrix there are many possible occasions when aims could be stated behaviourally in the 'FACTUAL KNOWLEDGE' and the 'PRACTICAL APPLICATION' columns across the top and in the categories down the left-hand side.

Serious practical drawbacks to stating aims in behavioural terms will be becoming clear to the reader. Do teachers have the time or the inclination to work out their behavioural objectives? Are there not a lot of instances where measurement is dubious, say in attitudes, dispositions and feelings, both from the moral point of view and from the availability of measures? If the teacher pre-specifies objectives, does this not prevent him or her from taking advantage of opportunities which may present themselves in the class-room? A teacher may have prepared a lesson thoroughly, only to find that a squabble breaks out, disrupting the lesson. In this situation a skilful teacher can use inductive methods to bring out important learning opportunities about friendship or relationships.

Faced with a class of children it is essential to have objectives, as well as lesson content, clearly worked out.

Another objection might be that we do not want to pre-specify outcomes, but may want to allow pupils the freedom to respond emotionally to a film about handicapped children, or to work out their own solution in a group drama situation to a problem about, say, 'getting home late'. Teachers may well wish to have much more open-ended aims.

Teachers may wish 'to develop a capacity for looking critically at values and beliefs, to weigh evidence and acquire standards of comparison and powers of discrimination', as one writer in Ken David's working party puts it. 'Development of understanding of society, of human relationships, of our own or other people's behaviour' cannot be specified in precise behavioural terms. Empathy and concern for others are not entities we possess, but attributes which can develop and grow. We may wish our young people to learn how to make decisions, but may not wish to say what their decisions should be in the realms of values, moral judgements, opinions and commitment in politics. This is where the process or procedural principles or aims are helpful.

I may wish to set up opportunities for discussion where ideas, attitudes, values and beliefs may be discussed, explored and debated, so that my pupils may come to a deeper understanding of the issues involved. I may wish to use the process of Values Clarification to help my pupils develop values through the use of games, pencil and paper exercises, or through simulations. Role play, the use of imagination through drama, literature and art may be processes through which children explore their feelings, gain insights or learn vicariously about social situations. The teacher may adopt processes or procedures in the class-room to enable particular kinds of understanding or skill to develop. In the case of political education, Bernard Crick suggests[4] that procedural values should be built into the class-room process—values such as freedom, toleration, fairness, respect for truth, and respect for reasoning—in order to bring about the political literacy he is advocating.

Lesley Button has developed process principles in his *Group Tutoring for the Form Tutor*.[5] He maintains that to be human is to be in relationship with other people, and that, 'in order to learn how to develop and maintain those relationships, a group of people must be available as an arena in which they can be learned and practised'. This developmental group work is a process of offering people opportunities for vital experiences with others through the membership of a group which is supportive and whose members are willing to help one another in personal ways. His source books are full of practical programmes and strategies for implementing these principles.

I believe teachers need more frequently to stop and think about this question, 'What are my aims?' It is true that experienced teachers can walk into a class-room where they have a warm relationship with the children, and say: 'All right, kids, what are we going to talk about today?' They can draw out whatever happens to be there. They can help the children clarify their ideas. They can offer alternative explanations, bring in different evidence for consideration, tell a story to illustrate a point, and so on.

What are they doing? They are working on a particular set of process principles derived from social psychologists (or perhaps from their own experience) on how to work with groups to explore their concerns and interests, and to exploit the power of the peer group. Teachers often operate on pedagogic principles in intuitive and unplanned ways. In fact our unplanned lessons are often the ones which seem most effective, or well-received. This is no excuse, though, for avoiding intelligent reflection about our work, particularly about our intentions, aims, principles of procedure, the processes we set up in the class-room. It is all too easy to teach for recall of facts and memorized explanations. These are low-level tasks which students find fairly straightforward. But is this really what Personal, Social and Moral Education is about?

A sharpening of critical and analytical thinking helps the teacher to reflect more carefully about aims. The concepts involved in our teaching are often the stumbling-block to understanding. We can be talking to young people in the most abstract terms about moral problems, or their self-esteem, and we wonder why they are not looking more interested! A second look at Piaget or Kohlberg might help us root our language in concrete, experiential situations. Any aims we have, any concepts we are trying to teach, any language used in the class-room, must take account of how the child's mind and experience develop, and of his normal use of language, which may be very different from our own.

At my own school, we have found it very useful to analyse the actual learning task of the child. What are we actually requiring of the child in our lessons? Does he/she know what to do? Does he know how to do it? Does he possess the logical skills to answer the question? Are there any difficult concepts lurking behind deceptively easy language? In Personal, Social and Moral Education, particularly, how does what we are asking him to do make him feel in front of the others?

These questions are important. Reflection about the school, its social setting, what our pupils are like, how they best learn, what they already know, understand and experience, is very useful background information when we begin to think seriously about what we are doing and why we do it. It could be argued that teachers have instinctive, intuitive, tacit knowledge of what they are doing through long experience of class-rooms, and therefore do not need to waste time elucidating their aims. I am sympathetic to that argument, because teaching should be seen as an art, or a craft, rather than simply a technology. However, I am convinced that systematic reflection about our practice, and especially aims, is the first step towards improving what we do.

Discussion about aims, purposes and processes relates very much to the earlier points I made about underlying assumptions and values in Personal, Social and Moral Education. If you have a particular iew of what people's personal and ocial lives should be, this will colour our approach to the aims of your work. All schools encourage articular virtues: kindness, olerance, respect for authority, bedience perhaps (teachers may nsist on this, even when they profess rogressive or liberal views of ducation). All these are commonly ngendered in our schools. Certain haracter traits are actively ncouraged in pastoral work: erseverance, initiative (not too much f it, though!), enterprise, creativity, esponsibility. At the back of every eacher's mind are the virtues and haracter traits which he or she avours. These will undoubtedly nfluence our aims in this work with hildren.

Some teachers feel that it is not heir business to influence the ubstantive personal choices and alues of pupils. They maintain we nust only set up procedures whereby upils can discuss, explore, determine and evaluate their own alues and beliefs. They argue that if ve try to get children to conform to rescribed socially acceptable goals, ve cannot escape the charge of ndoctrination. In reality I think it is lifficult for a school *not* to foster articular values, virtues and haracter attributes. Our Personal, ocial and Moral Education lessons an provide a forum where these alues are examined, challenged and liscussed by the pupils.

It is very useful to distinguish two rocesses. The first is the school ublicly stating what it cherishes, vhat values it holds. The second is he students' own understanding of hese values, coming to terms with hem, challenging them, evaluating hem personally, and choosing their wn values. In my school the astoral programme fosters the first rocess, and the social education rogramme encourages the second, lthough there is of course a lot of verlap.

This brings me to the relationship etween the aims of the Personal, ocial and Moral Education rogramme and the over-all aims of he school. I frequently meet teachers vho are introducing innovatory rogrammes whose aims and

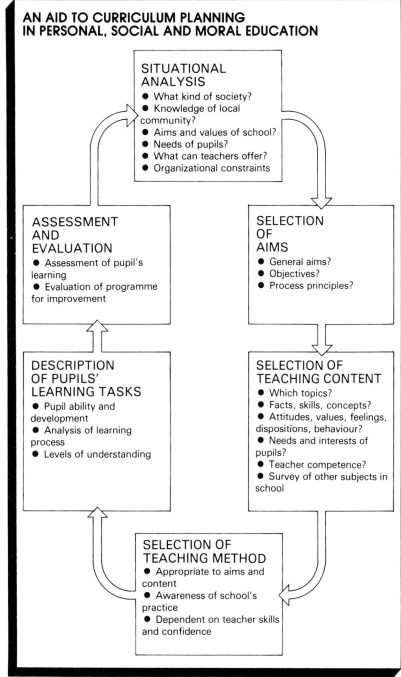

processes are not in harmony with the values and aims of their school. This gives rise to several problems and conflicts. I remember, when I first began to teach in this area at my present school, how fearful senior colleagues were that these new (and as they thought liberal) ideas might undermine the authority of the

school or distract children's attention from the main purpose of school— which they believed to be passing examinations. These fears were, of course, unfounded, because the programme I introduced was matched to the philosophy of the senior management.

Consider, though, a school where

pupils have been conditioned to think compliantly, where the emphasis is on conformity to a particular set of values. If a young teacher were to develop in his pupils independent reasoning, questioning, the clarification of values, there might well be trouble for those same students if they exercised these skills in an authoritarian class-room. It might be very uncomfortable for teachers used to decanting knowledge to their pupils to have them question the relevance of that knowledge!

Or consider a teacher introducing moral reasoning to a class, attempting to raise the moral development of his students to a higher level of justice reasoning, in a school where decisions which affected student interests were made on instrumental grounds, or for the self-interest of the management. All kinds of tensions and cynicism about moral reasoning could arise in young minds. Young people are very quick to observe the gap between precept and practice, the apparent or real hypocrisy in a school. Wherever possible the stated aims of the Personal, Social and Moral Education programme should match those of the school.

I have often been asked at conferences if teachers should give up, where this match is not possible. (Younger colleagues often feel discouraged when they are developing aspects of this area.) My answer is 'No'. Personal, Social and Moral Education is too important to give up. These aspects of development take place with or without our conscious help. We can promote growth, or we can hinder and distort it. I think, on balance,

that teachers should develop programmes of work for their pupils only after consultations with senior colleagues about their aims and methods. Schools need integrated, planned, whole curricula, not splintered and autonomous parts. I am sure our work is much more effective where there is this integrated match between school values and what the individual does in his or her class-room. Where this is not possible it is still worthwhile to beaver away on our own, and perhaps try to change things by reason and discussion.

I have two practical suggestions which may be helpful in working out aims.

● The first is to look back at the matrix in chapter two and try to plot the social aims of our school. Is it more concerned with autonomy, individualism and independence, or with collaboration, group co-operation and community? Is it the main drift of school policy to induct the pupils into particular socially-acceptable forms of behaviour, to reproduce or inculcate the best virtues, dispositions and behaviour that society has to offer? Perhaps the emphasis is more on changing the inequalities in society, solving the problems of the local community.

I have tried plotting schools on this matrix. It is difficult to decide in which quarter they should go, but the process has helped clarify the social aims of the schools in question.

Most of the projects or approaches I have surveyed in this book spell out their aims or process principles. It is instructive to read them.

● Then I would suggest planning a

lesson with clear behavioural objectives. Teach the lesson. Get a friendly colleague to observe it or tape-record it. Reflect about how effective you think it was. Do not be too critical of yourself. Then plan a lesson on the same or a similar topic using procedural aims, process principles. Teach the lesson. Compare the two.

I have found this an effective way of sorting out the two approaches and highlighting the importance of aims.

If you cannot think of appropriate process principles, try using the Values Clarification strategies I mentioned in chapter three, or the Kohlberg dilemma methodology. Suitable topics might be 'stealing', 'smoking', or 'the skill of listening'.

If only we would stop more frequently and ask ourselves:
● Why am I doing this?
● What do I hope to achieve?
the learning process would be much more effective. Our aims, our principles of planning lead us to consider the methods we use, class-room materials, and the nature of the learning task we give to our pupils.

Footnotes

1. An Open University set book.
2. R. Tyler, *Basic Principles of Curriculum and Instruction*.
3. Kenneth David, *Personal and Social Education in Secondary Schools*.
4. Bernard Crick, Alex Porter (eds.), *Political Education and Political Literacy*.
5. L. Button, *Group Tutoring for the Form Tutor*.

CHAPTER 6

PLANNING PRINCIPLES:
THE CONTENT

At a meeting of senior staff at my school we reviewed our pastoral education programme and our Social Education. We sat down together to make a list of all the topics we thought should be covered. After two meetings we had agreed a list without too much trouble. I would guess that any group of teachers with experience in Personal, Social and Moral Education would find it a relatively simple task to come to a large measure of agreement about what topics might be covered.

This might not be the case in a school which is introducing a structured programme, reviewing the existing arrangements with a view to change, or where teachers have controlled particular areas of the curriculum—say in Home Economics, Religious Education or Biology—and are reluctant to see change. (Some of these organizational problems are covered in chapter seven.) However, more widely among educators (both theoreticians and practitioners), there is a large measure of agreement about the content of what might count as Personal, Social and Moral Education.

Some local education authorities in England have published guidebooks on this area for teachers. Lancashire published a very helpful guidebook in the 1970s entitled *Pastoral Work and Education in Personal Relationships in Lancashire Secondary Schools.* This has an immense check-list, nine pages long, of themes for courses in Education for Personal Relationships, Family Life Education, Social and Personal Development, Moral and Social Education, Personal Guidance and Health Education. Bedfordshire published a discussion paper on Health Education in 1980 which contains lists of suitable topics for various ages of children. Berkshire, Sussex and Devon are three more local education authorities which I know have published their own guidebooks. They all contain a number of common threads.

I have already referred to a number of guidebooks, practical teaching materials, projects and approaches of which I have some personal knowledge. Among the topics covered, a number of themes keep recurring. The newer pastoral or tutorial programmes also have similar themes, although these may be slanted more towards life and problems related to school and learning.

What are these common themes?

● The first is *self-awareness, self-esteem,* and *self-assessment.* This theme runs through the health education projects, through the clarification materials, and in the tutorial programmes. Careers education programmes often include this as a major theme. There seem to be several sources of this interest: Biological Science and Community Medicine; Humanistic Psychology and the Human Potential Movement's influence on education; and the impact of self-assessment in careers counselling. I suspect that the approaches to Religious Education in the 1960s and 70s in the UK— sometimes called the 'implicit approach'—has influenced class-room work on self-awareness, personal values and beliefs.

● The wide area of *health education* is another theme: hygiene, information on which health choices can be made, diseases, risks to health, and mental health or positive well-being. This concept of health is not only preventive, but much wider and more positive, as I have pointed out in an earlier chapter. The content of the health dimension may vary in different societies where there are special needs. Urban society may need an emphasis on the dangers of obesity, on exercise, industrial diseases, or environmental health. A rural community in, say, a particular Third World country may emphasize nutrition, the elimination of a particular disease, family planning, or the water supply.

● *Education in personal relationships* is a dominant theme. Learning how to 'get on' with people is an essential part of human life: relations in the family, friendships, co-operating in groups, boy-girl friendships, coming to terms with authority in the home, school, with local community leaders, in working life and in wider society with the law and the police. Learning how to cope with people and the demands they make, learning how to cherish the most helpful people in my life; learning about how people communicate through tone of voice, gesture and symbol, and facial expressions—these are all important aspects of personal relationships.

Many children, particularly in adolescence, find difficulty with these skills: how to keep friends; how to meet and talk with strangers; accepted social skills, manners and customs in strange situations; how to 'date' a person of the opposite sex; what to do in a crowded place; how to cope with loneliness, frustration, anxiety; how to sort out, or come to terms with, our feelings about people; or how to solve personal problems. Personal relationships is a very wide area and is often broken-up in syllabuses under titles such as 'friendship', 'sex', 'the family', 'school', 'marriage', 'intolerance', 'leisure', 'work', 'authority', 'freedom and responsibility', 'behaviour', and so on. Undoubtedly children are very interested and concerned about their personal relationships.

• A fourth common, but controversial theme is *sex education* which might include human physiology, the onset of puberty, human reproduction, human sexuality, the birth and care of babies, family planning, venereal diseases, and sex and the law. Education for family life, the sociology of the family, the human relationship aspects of sex such as dating, petting, making love, the exploration of feelings, problems in friendships, might also be included. Preparation for marriage, choosing a partner, chastity versus licence in sexual relationships, child development and parenthood might be included for senior pupils.

Much controversy centres on such questions as 'To what extent has the state (or other adults) the right to encroach on what should be a private family affair?', and: 'How can parents be sure that such delicate personal and moral areas of life will be taught with either the sensitivity or the value assumptions of which they will approve?'

There is no doubt in my mind that the home is the proper place for sex education. Where home life is fragmented, where relationships are torn—then there is a case for schools working out a careful programme of sex education. Guiding principles should be: co-operation with parents, implying consent; sensitivity to the feelings of the children; appropriateness of aspects of content to the age and development of the pupils; and the underlying value assumption of responsibility.

Teachers in state schools might like to test these principles against their experience as sex educators, to relate them to what schools are doing, and to decide whether they agree. You may wish to set up different procedural values of your own. Christians working in private schools would certainly want to add further principles or values, such as chastity, the New Testament teaching on marriage, divorce, family relationships.

In practice it is very difficult to

avoid the subject of sex in a secondary school! It is a legitimate part of courses in Human Biology or Sociology. The subject presents itself to teachers in girl-boy relationships, through the media, advertising, graffiti on toilet walls. And pupils in adolescence have a natural interest and curiosity. Along with other values issues, a school needs to hammer out its policy on sex education and make it public.

• Most approaches to Personal, Social and Moral Education have *ethical* or *behavioural* content. This may be the teaching of moral thinking or reasoning; the acquiring of empathic skills (the ability to put yourself in another's shoes); the practice or discussion of how to consider, or why to care about, others; or the encouragement or inculcation of particular virtues, character traits, attitudes or dispositions. Most teachers I meet are very concerned about the way pupils should or should not behave. Principles of conduct, the regulation of behaviour, beliefs about right and wrong, the formation of values in pupils, the consideration of various views about controversial human issues—all appear regularly in pastoral or tutorial work, or in Religious Education, Humanities, Social Studies, or in syllabuses concerned with this wider area of the curriculum about personal, social and moral development.

As we discussed earlier, there are a number of different approaches to the moral, ethical or behavioural area of the curriculum both in what the content should be and in the methods or class-room processes. When the basic philosophy and aims of this work have been decided, the content can be arrived at and the process or procedural principles can be established. The reader will decide for himself which approach to moral education he favours. The questions that follow may help with the decision-making process about content and process:

1. What is moral education about? Is it more the inculcating of particular virtues and discouragement of undesirable behaviour, or is it concerned with

introducing children to morality as a distinct form of thought or experience?

2. What kind of behaviours, attitudes, dispositions, and beliefs would the staff of your school, the parents of the pupils, and the wider community wish to see in the children? What behaviours are most conducive to the educational aims of the school?

3. What are the moral skills children need in order to cope with the plurality of views about the moral life? What are the questions, the concerns and interests of our pupils in the 'moral' area of life? What are the big moral questions that affect their experience, present and future?

Readers will have their own particular stance on the question of what the moral content should be. These questions may help to clarify thinking. I have already declared my own position in this book.

• *Economic* and *industrial awareness* and *Careers Education* might be considered separately in their own right. But there is overlap with other areas mentioned here. A reasonable knowledge of the working of the economy, the structure and function of industry, and an understanding of skills required for participation in employment find a place in many Careers Education courses. Then there is the information and counselling function about job opportunities, training schemes, and further and higher education, work experience schemes, and preparation for applications and interviews for jobs, and information about unemployment, national insurance and taxation which many Careers departments give young people.

Decision-making and social skills are often taught. Life-skills, self-assessment in preparation for choosing school subjects, and later for employment, are taught in many Careers lessons in English schools, alongside topics about saving, mortgages, banking, keeping simple accounts and budgeting. Careers advice and counselling has needed much rethinking with the growth of unemployment. There is much common ground between Careers

Education and what I have designated Personal, Social and Moral Education—indeed in my own local authority the two appear to be almost synonymous.

● Closely related to work, industry and economics is *Political Education*. Children should surely be given help to understand their own country's constitution, its government at local and national levels, and how the laws are made. At the age of majority we expect young people to make informed choices about local and national politics. What are schools doing to prepare them for voting? Political literacy is more than just giving information about how the country is run, or about the beliefs of the major political parties. There is hardly an area of our lives that is not affected by political policies or decisions.

I find that pupils are seldom interested in politics before the age of sixteen unless they can be helped to experience and discuss political concepts and action such as 'authority', 'force', 'decision-making', 'influence and persuasion', 'power', 'responsibility' and so on. If we can help pupils understand these and other concepts, as B. Crick and A. Porter suggest, if we can help them enter into 'politicizing' by games, simulations, through a schools council or by discussion, debate and decision-making about their own affairs or social events, we will have more success in our attempts to help them understand what the political world is all about. The micro-political process in their lives, families, friendships, school, youth clubs, and the exploration of themes which arouse interest—such as 'housing', 'street violence', 'poverty', the Cruise missile debate, 'racism' and 'unemployment'—seem to be the most successful approaches in my own school.

● Linked with Political Education is the general contribution of the *social sciences* to Personal, Social and Moral Education. Topics such as 'inequality', 'the family', 'population', 'education', 'mass media', 'social order, functions and structures', and 'social problems'

such as poverty, racism, old age and urbanization, often appear in syllabuses. 'Social institutions', 'the study of groups', studies of 'different kinds of societies', and 'a multi-cultural society' also frequently appear. I come across comments from social scientists criticizing the intellectual rigour and discipline of Personal, Social and Moral Education. No doubt our courses would benefit by more insights and concepts from Sociology, Anthropology and Social Psychology. I have noticed a lot more emphasis on social skills training in recent publications, particularly in connection with the Youth Training Schemes.

● *Safety* and *survival* is another theme. Many schools cover topics such as road safety, first-aid, safety in school—including the laboratory, the sports field, the gymnasium, swimming-pool, around the school, 'where to get help and when'—and wider safety issues: in the home; in public buildings; what to do if you see an accident or a fire.

World problems such as 'race', 'overpopulation', 'hunger', 'rivalry between political ideologies', 'the nuclear arms race', and topics such as the 'United Nations', the 'Third World', 'overseas aid', 'human rights', and various relief and helping organizations appear in the World

Group work involving both discussion and decision-making play an important part in the learning process.

Studies sections of these courses, or arise out of discussion about current affairs.

Environmental and *ecological issues*—from 'broken glass in the school playing-field' to major concerns such as 'the rape of natural resources' or 'the altering of the balance of nature' play an important part in many programmes. Many of these topics are studied elsewhere in the curriculum, in sciences and humanities.

I have no doubt that there are areas I have omitted that the reader will wish to add. The space I have given to each theme should not be interpreted as a comment on its importance. I have noted these themes as those most commonly recurring in publications and schemes of work I have looked at.

● The final theme I want to draw attention to is that of *the school*. Information about staffing, organization, homework, uniform, rules, bounds, what is expected of pupils, where they can get help for various problems, timing, and equipment—endless information is needed by the children for them to cope with the demands of school life. To be successful pupils they need to know not only information, but skills too: how to follow their timetable, organize themselves for the day, bring the right books and equipment, plan their leisure and homework, and choose the right subjects when the time comes. There are critical incidents in their school life; study skills they need to acquire to be successful learners; techniques in preparing for and answering examination questions; skills in relating to other people in the hurly-burly of the playground, the dinner queue, or the class-room. No matter how resilient children are, there is no doubt that the Personal, Social and Moral Education programme can do much to help them. A school's pastoral care can make a tremendous difference, not only to the welfare of its pupils, but to effective learning.

There is always a danger of writing out lists of content that teachers should cover in their lessons, without thinking long and hard about our aims. Lists of topics by themselves are insufficient. We need to break down the content into concepts and cognitive capacities, into attitudes, feelings and dispositions, as well as

into the facts to be known. If our planning is effective we will think about the particular skills we wish children to acquire, and the practical application of the knowledge.

The ability to put into practise the decision-making skills, the moral thinking, the communication skills, the insights into personal relationships, may be more important than the knowledge itself. The ability to make moral decisions, the *practice* of responsibility, or whatever it is we are trying to teach, is more important than *knowing* how to do it—and not carrying it out. This is, of course, why opportunities should be made in lessons for children to practise and apply what is taught.

We do not want the content of our lessons to be memorized, or simply reconstructed in their own words. We want the lesson itself to be a *process* of practising the thinking, acquiring and doing the skill, relating the knowledge to an area of the pupils' life, clarifying their values, learning to build self-esteem—or, in the case of community service or work experience, going out and actually experiencing the social

problem—the practice of caring or responsibility. The content may be of potential interest, but there is always a danger that it will remain external to the pupil's inner life.

Like many teachers, I am accused by my pupils of being boring. (Usually they say the lesson is boring, putting it more politely!) Often, what they mean is that the content of the lesson is not touching something real for them. We cannot always do this. A lot of disciplined hard work may be necessary before they reach understanding—and then interest comes. Motivation is not a new problem to the class teacher! However, the teacher of Personal, Social and Moral Education needs to take the motivation problem—the question of the child's interest—very seriously. The child should be at the centre of what we are doing. Furthermore, there should be a link between the child's development and the content of the lesson. This may be all 'old hat' to the experienced teacher, but I find I need constantly to remind myself of developmental psychology, to re-read child-development books, to look again at

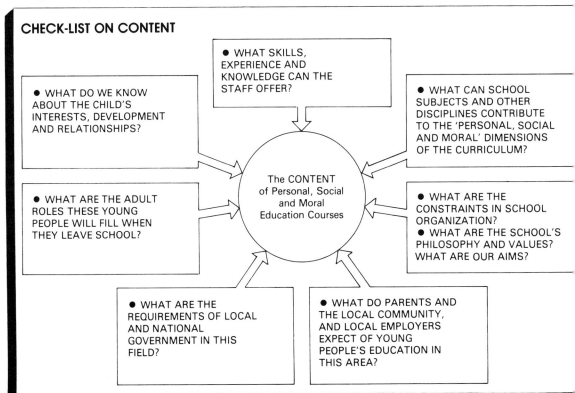

CHECK-LIST ON CONTENT

● WHAT SKILLS, EXPERIENCE AND KNOWLEDGE CAN THE STAFF OFFER?

● WHAT DO WE KNOW ABOUT THE CHILD'S INTERESTS, DEVELOPMENT AND RELATIONSHIPS?

● WHAT CAN SCHOOL SUBJECTS AND OTHER DISCIPLINES CONTRIBUTE TO THE 'PERSONAL, SOCIAL AND MORAL' DIMENSIONS OF THE CURRICULUM?

The CONTENT of Personal, Social and Moral Education Courses

● WHAT ARE THE ADULT ROLES THESE YOUNG PEOPLE WILL FILL WHEN THEY LEAVE SCHOOL?

● WHAT ARE THE CONSTRAINTS IN SCHOOL ORGANIZATION?
● WHAT ARE THE SCHOOL'S PHILOSOPHY AND VALUES? WHAT ARE OUR AIMS?

● WHAT ARE THE REQUIREMENTS OF LOCAL AND NATIONAL GOVERNMENT IN THIS FIELD?

● WHAT DO PARENTS AND THE LOCAL COMMUNITY, AND LOCAL EMPLOYERS EXPECT OF YOUNG PEOPLE'S EDUCATION IN THIS AREA?

the pupils' mental development, and ask myself: *Is my lesson content appropriate to the pupils I teach?*

Often I assume it is, but on closer thought or discussion with the children I find it is not. In Personal, Social and Moral Education this may be more vital than in other areas of the curriculum. At my school we consult with the pupils, asking them about their interests, what they have found most helpful, how they think the work could be improved.

The topics I have noted will have connections with other areas of the curriculum. Geographers, Biologists, Religious Educationalists, English Literature specialists, may all fear that part of their cherished course is being devoured by the new PSME monster! I have attended curriculum planning meetings where there has been genuine concern about overlap, or about non-specialists dealing with a specialist topic in an inaccurate way. Teachers who feel that a particular topic is central to their subject do not want others poaching or 'messing about' with it. I shall deal with problems of co-ordination, overlap, whole curriculum planning and other organizational issues in the next chapter.

Before I leave the question of *content* I want to consider the question many Christian teachers raise: 'Is there any special "Christian" content in Personal, Social and Moral Education?' I believe there is, as I argued in chapter 4, a legitimate right to put forward Christian views on controversial issues alongside other views. There is the special contribution of Christian self-giving love to pastoral care. There is the distinctive contribution of Christian 'salvation-wholeness' which Christian teachers will want to share with their pupils for their consideration. The uniqueness of Christian claims in the area of spiritual and personal, social and moral development can also be discussed and evaluated as far as the children are able. The imposition of one view is not education as I understand it. At any point where questions of value are under

discussion it is legitimate to express the Christian viewpoint. Questions of 'ought' or 'should', 'right' or 'the best' involve values, opinions and beliefs. So where we are teaching about questions of right and wrong, attributes in pupils, behaviour, personal relationships, beliefs, there will be Christian views to explore, as well as humanist, Muslim, liberal, or Marxist views.

I will take two topics as examples, to illustrate how a Christian teacher might contribute 'special' or 'extra' content.

● What might the Christian contribution be on the themes of 'self-awareness', 'self-esteem' and 'self-assessment' which appear frequently in courses? Christian teachers might want to refer to ideas about the 'nature of man', made in the image of God, to account for the 'creative' and 'ingenious', the 'noble and self-sacrificing' ideas and deeds of people. The concept of 'sin' and 'evil' could also be introduced in relation to moral problems, evil in society, or our own potential for evil. Christians might want to make the point that self-fulfilment is realized in the Christian faith by self-sacrifice and service to others. Our own identity is realized as we function in the Christian community as part of the 'body of Christ'.

Living at peace with myself, the realistic assessment of my ability, and the 'priceless worth' of my individuality, are all found in Christianity. The New Testament makes many references to 'acceptance', 'repentance', 'being loved', 'chosen'—all of which build self-esteem. Some qualities of character are condemned, others are commended. Christianity is certainly interested in 'kind of persons', character traits and behaviour. Theological ideas which are central to the Christian faith have direct relation to self-awareness. The creation, the atonement, the incarnation, redemption, the church, salvation, eternal life: all these themes have something to say about 'the self'. This is only the briefest of surveys. The link between self-

esteem and allied concepts, and Christian theology, could be expanded at length.

● The thoughtful reader will also see that Christians have deep insights to bring to themes of personal relationships. The New Testament contains general principles of human relationships, and specific guidance about particulars. The great principle of 'Love your neighbour as yourself' and the golden rule, 'Do to others as you would wish them to do to you', immediately spring to mind. Reconciliation is a major biblical theme. Paul urges us to 'put on' particular virtues in our relationships, and to 'put off' others. The 'fruit of the Spirit', the 'works of the flesh', and detailed help with the family, marriage, and church relationships will be familiar to readers of Paul's letters. The Old Testament book of Proverbs is full of sayings about human relationships.

The Bible offers light and help on almost any theme in the field of personal relationships: friendship; anger; love; loyalty; sexual relationships; marriage; divorce; authority; family life; feelings about people; communication; encouragement; reconciliation; nurturing relationships—the list is endless. I need not develop the point further.

I would like to encourage Christian teachers to take any theme which falls within the content of Personal, Social and Moral Education and develop what they might consider as 'Christian content' on issues of a controversial, or values nature. Most of the themes mentioned in this chapter have possibilities. Simply ask yourself the question: *What does the Bible, or the church, have to say about this theme?* I believe that Christian teachers should not deny their pupils the opportunity of knowing what Christ has to say.

Footnote

1. B. Crick, A. Porter (eds.), *Political Education and Political Literacy*.

CHAPTER 7

PLANNING PRINCIPLES: THE ORGANIZATION

The topics and skills listed in the previous chapter for the content of Personal, Social and Moral Education raise questions about organization.

Where should these topics and skills appear in the school curriculum?

Is this a new subject we are introducing?

How does the content relate to existing disciplines and subjects?

Will there be overlap, or poaching of favourite topics?

We cannot have RE, Biology, Home Economics, Social Studies, Humanities and English Literature all dealing with sex, race, the family, and leisure, can we?

'Who is going to sort this lot out?' I hear somebody saying. 'We all seem to be hiring the same "Trigger" films and using the same educational videos.'

'Haven't we had enough innovation and change recently?'

And a more cynical old chalk may comment, 'We had all this before, and we've seen these hybrids wither and die in the class-room heat.'

Realists will want to work out some answers to these questions. In this chapter I offer some thoughts which may help with some of these organizational problems.

There are four clearly identifiable views about organization which I have heard expressed by teachers or seen in print.

● First there is the *adversary view*. There are teachers who believe that personal, social and moral development are not the legitimate concern of teachers. They complain they have not been trained as social workers, or feel they should not be quasi-psychologists or priests. Sometimes adversary views are expressed differently: 'This area is

far too controversial. Questions of value are not my concern. I deal in what is known and publicly recognized as knowledge. Leave values and personal development to parents and the church. We have no right to interfere.' I have frequently heard the comment: 'Leave this airy-fairy stuff alone. Get them through their exams. That is what education is about!'

We can engage the adversary view in argument. We can attempt to justify the place of Personal, Social and Moral Education, as I tried to do in chapter 2. Some adversaries dig their heels in even deeper, but many teachers will be convinced by gentle and persistent reason along these lines: '*Loco parentis* demands attention to this area and, in any case, we do influence the pupil's development. Is it not better to plan for this element of development rather than let it happen in an unplanned and haphazard way?'

● The second view I have met is that we need not make any special effort in this area because it is happening already, naturally, through Literature, Humanities, Music, Art, Science, History, RE, visits abroad, residentials and even assemblies . . . This I have called the *fragmented view*.

The school atmosphere, its values, its philosophy, its pastoral care, all infuse aspects of personal, social and moral development into the lives of the pupils. Add to this the specific content: the skills, the concepts, the experiences that the distinctive subjects give through their normal work in the class-room and it all adds up to a very respectable Personal, Social and Moral Education. You do not have to concern yourself with integrated courses, collaborative planning, pastoral or tutorial

programmes because 'it is all happening anyway'.

I have tried not to parody this view because there is a lot of good sense and practical wisdom here. Many adults are perfectly well adjusted without having had special courses in personal relationships. Many schools deal very effectively with this area of education through the normal curriculum, their pastoral care, and informally through the wider extra-curricular activities of the school. We can all quote RE departments, Home Economics teachers, English teachers, Drama specialists, or school orchestras where imaginative, sensitive and influential work is going on in this field. My only concern about this view is that there are so many different subject areas becoming more aware of this field, that, unless we have some co-operation and co-ordination among different specialists, irritating problems will arise. We may have carefully planned a series of lessons on health, only to be told by a pert 13-year-old: 'Oh, that's boring . . . we've seen this film in Science and Home Economics—and Mr so-and-so showed it us too, when Miss S— was away ill.' All your careful planning principles! Also the more splintered or segmented approach can lead to no one really knowing what aspects of this area are being taught, by whom, when and where. It is too important to be left to this fragmented, haphazard treatment.

● The third approach, which is becoming increasingly popular, is where a group of colleagues get together and work out a course for a particular group. This co-operative and collaborative approach I call the *integrated view*. When problems arise subject departments co-operate at various levels.

When I taught in Birmingham as an RE specialist we found that there was overlap between the Biology and RE courses with 15-year-olds in sex education. The teachers concerned defended and argued at first, but then came to an amicable agreement about which department should teach particular aspects. This was co-operation at a simple level.

During the period of preparation just before the raising of the school-leaving age in England I was teaching in Reading. A group of teachers in the Humanities and Science departments, together with other interested colleagues, spent many hours discussing ways of teaching these older young people with whom we would have to deal. We were trying to take account of their interests, and attempting to prepare them for adult roles when they left school at the new age of sixteen. We overcame traditional subject boundaries and planned a course of work which drew on the skills and knowledge of the teachers which they could contribute to given themes and topics as individuals in a team.

This team-teaching approach had what was called 'lead lessons' or 'key lessons' given by a specialist to a group of 150–200 pupils. Other teachers joined in where appropriate, adding their insights. The pupils then went to smaller classes and pursued work prepared by the specialist for the other teachers. There was flexibility for musical, dramatic, and quiz-type input from teachers with particular skills. One colleague had a great sense of humour, another an interest in community service, another had group counselling skills: all these were utilized at various times. We had regular planning meetings and frequently had to make our own written learning resources. It was exciting and rewarding work, but demanded a lot of time and energy.

Unfortunately, integrated approaches to Personal, Social and Moral Education are for the less able or troublesome pupils in many schools. The implicit assumption is that brighter children do better with an extra language or science subject. One wonders, though, whether the

extra subjects promote personal, social and moral development in brighter children. I reject the view that this education is somehow to fill up what is lacking through intelligence or social background. A 'deficit model' of social or moral education is at best doubtful and questionable—and appears erroneous and arrogant in its more extreme forms. Fortunately curriculum development projects and educational publications of late have done a lot to discourage this deficit view. I fear it may be resurrected. Personal, social and moral development should not be considered as only for deficit (or elite) groups of children—whatever those doubtful terms mean. It is necessary for *all* children.

● This leads me to the fourth approach to organization which I designate the *whole curriculum view*. The *Lifeline* project encouraged curriculum planners to take note of how various subjects across the curriculum could contribute to moral education. More recently the Health Education Project 13–18 encourages schools to review the provision the curriculum as a whole is making for the wider health education of the pupils. In the Co-ordinator's Guide there is advice and help on how to design a matrix of topics and subjects to plot the various elements in particular subjects at given ages.

Kenneth David, in the Schools Council Programme 3 publication,[1] sets aside a chapter to developing a whole curriculum or co-ordinated programme. I strongly recommend this chapter (chapter five) to the reader. Mr David writes from long experience of these matters and his practical wisdom shines through. *Active Tutorial Work*, which I have already mentioned several times, advocates a co-ordinated approach to areas of this work through the pastoral work of the school.

While I can understand the misgivings and opposition of some colleagues to Personal, Social and Moral Education, while I can see much value in single subjects or individual teachers making their separate contribution, I believe there is much more value in the collaborative approaches or integrated courses. By far the best

approach in terms of over-all effectiveness is the whole curriculum approach, in my opinion. It is not my place to tell others how to organize their work—I simply offer the reader some points about the benefits and merits of a whole curriculum approach for consideration. These points are illustrated from experience at Rotheram High School, Luton.

The whole curriculum approach is where the leaders of a school believe in the importance of personal, social and moral development and are prepared to make time for this work within the timetable. The aims of this work should be supported by the philosophy of the school. When I was appointed in 1975 to co-ordinate Social Education I had the necessary support and the position, power and authority from the head to do the work. I spent my first year teaching my subject, but also consulting each head of department and examining syllabuses to see how much of this aspect of education was already going on in the school. I found that there was a great deal: in English, Science, Careers, Religious Education, Home Economics, Technical Studies, Mathematics and in the pastoral care and extra-curricular activities. I drew up a matrix to show which topics appeared in the over-all curriculum. I then began to construct courses, first with 11–12-year-olds, then with 15-year-olds. Later, with the help of several colleagues, we designed courses for all pupils of all abilities throughout the school.

First we looked at the whole curriculum, then we planned courses to avoid duplication, overlap, and haphazard organization. We wanted all children to benefit—not only those who happened to take an excellent optional subject such as 'Child Development' in their fourth year. This whole curriculum approach is described in Ken David's book, and in more detail in a paper, 'Social Education at Rotheram High School . . . An innovation . . . some recollections . . . and some reflections', which is available from the school in Luton. It has taken a long time to reach our present state. There are still many problems to solve, things to improve. We still have not 'got it right'. A co-ordinator can be appointed on a high scale of salary to innovate, to convince others of the worth of the enterprise and to take the considerable strain.

An alternative whole curriculum approach is where a group of staff argues the case for a curriculum review. Here the group, rather than an individual, convinces the senior staff that an appraisal of the curriculum might be an appropriate way of ascertaining the extent of the present provision for personal, social and moral development. A review of what each subject contributes will yield a matrix, or a written description of the aspects each department contributes at particular ages in the children, From this review a picture of the present state will emerge, and decisions can be made about co-ordination, about duplication or overlap, about absences or gaps in topics or skills in particular groups, and about any necessary re-scheduling. I know of several schools which have adopted this approach.

The merits and benefits of this whole curriculum approach will be apparent to the reader. In the first place it is possible to avoid overlap of topics, duplication in the teaching of skills, the ordering of similar or the same written, or audio-visual aids. Key topics or skills and favourite themes will not be spoilt by other teachers pinching cherished material! All this can be properly sorted out, argued about, agreed, protected and co-ordinated. Futhermore, where there are topics drawing on insights from various disciplines (such as the family, law, relationships between people, and, say, animal rights), each discipline can contribute a particular view at a given time to illuminate the subject more effectively for the pupil.

The co-ordinated approach should improve organization, and it should show the learner that knowledge is not fragmented into isolated subjects. There is much merit in a more rounded view of education, seeing how the parts relate to the whole. With this approach we can make some attempt at finding out what is being taught. We can have a picture of what the school is trying to do in this area of education, and make

some attempt at evaluating the work. With the other, more splintered and haphazard approaches, much excellent work goes on but who knows what, and where, and with whom? Many children miss out extensively.

Each school will need to work out its own salvation here, with much debate and discussion. Decisions may need to be made about the use of tutorial periods, of a core curriculum containing Personal, Social and Moral Education, and of the planned contributions of individual subjects.

I helped at a staff conference of a Roman Catholic school recently where they had decided to make more constructive use of extended form periods or tutorial time for personal, social and moral development in their pupils.

I have had discussions with a school that has developed a common curriculum of English, Mathematics, Science, Technical Studies and Design, Humanities, Art and Craft, and Languages; what they call Social Education is taken by the form tutors throughout the school during timetabled time. There are all sorts of problems and constraints in this approach. Not all schools are ready for such a radical rethink, and perhaps need to try out a pilot scheme first. However, *if this area of school life is as important as this book claims, we need to review what schools are doing and ask if they are taking this work seriously.* The whole curriculum approach is the most effective attempt of the four to provide a co-ordinated, planned systematic and coherent Personal, Social and Moral Education for all the pupils of a school.

There is, of course, a whole literature about change and innovation, about the micro-politics of major social changes, or organizational changes in institutions. The literature abounds with rich metaphors such as 'band-wagon or hearse?', 'organizational health', 'tissue rejection' and 'Stone-Age obstructionists'. (Interested readers will find further references in the appendices.) I want to mention some of the real problems, constraints —and some helpful strategies—which I have come across, for making

progress in the organization of this work.

First of all there is the *conservatism of teachers*. Change usually means a disturbance in the security of the familiar. Often, in schools, change means extra work for colleagues, rethinking, the unfamiliar, and what has been called de-skilling. De-skilling involves giving people new tasks which demand new skills, rather than the familiar ones in which they already have expertise. Any agent for change needs to take the feelings of colleagues into consideration.

Are there any strategies for overcoming this conservatism—other than power-coercive? Readers might like to consider the notion of *practicality*. Teachers are busy people and essentially practical. An innovation which is imposed in a power-coercive way, may be in danger of failing altogether, or of being implemented only half-heartedly because, ironically, even though teachers are very conscious of their authority over children and depend on delegated authority, they can themselves be strongly anti-authority and often resent being told what to do. If we can demonstrate that the changes are practical, have merit, have useful outcomes, if the changes benefit the teacher and fulfil their needs and desires, they are much more likely to succeed. Rational and empirical arguments may help, but practicality is a key to success.

Another useful notion is *collaboration and participation*. I have found colleagues much more likely actually to change and implement new ideas, rather than simply go through the motions, if they are actively involved in making decisions about change. Commitment to a line of action is invariably deeper when the participant has taken part in the decision-making process. Many senior members of staff want to make organizational changes in Personal, Social and Moral Education but come to grief in the management of

The whole curriculum approach provides a co-ordinated and coherent Personal, Social and Moral Education for all pupils.

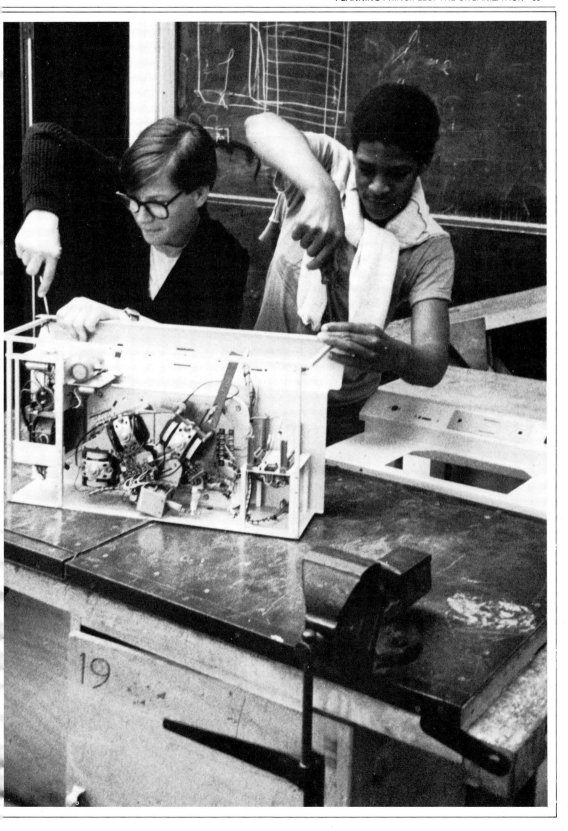

change. The notions of 'practicality', 'collaboration' and 'participation' are good starting-points for a more successful strategy of change.

Before schools begin to innovate on a large scale there are *practical organizational* issues which need airing and resolving. Questions about 'Who?', 'What?', 'When?', 'How?' and 'Where?' need answering. The 'Who?' involves not only *which* staff, and whether they are going to work as volunteers or be directed, but also the question of how suitable they are for this kind of work.

Some colleagues are well suited by training and personality to the matters of fact in Personal, Social and Moral Education, but are much less happy or competent to handle pupil opinion, questions of beliefs, values and attitudes. Many teachers are effective communicators in an instructional or expositional mode o

THE CO-ORDINATOR OF SOCIAL EDUCATION

The following paper was prepared by Rotheram High School, advertising for a senior member of staff to co-ordinate work in personal and social education. Whilst each school will differ in its style and needs, this paper may be of interest.

Social education

Social education covers those aspects of school life which contribute to the process of growing up, getting on with other people, the formation of values, and the preparation of the child for responsibility in adult life. This includes helping pupils to understand themselves, their behaviour, health and development, and to understand our society. It also includes helping children to understand their school, and to learn effectively. We try to teach them how to make decisions and moral judgements; we encourage them to be sensitive to their environment and to the beliefs and behaviour of others; and we try to foster an awareness of the major problems facing mankind.

Aspects of social education are found in the home, in various lessons in school, through the pastoral organization, and in the way people behave towards each other in school; but we have also organized courses for each year group in which topics suitable for the age, development and interest of the pupils are explored.

Introduction

1. The successful applicant will be committed to the philosophy of the school, and to the notion of social education as we understand it. Social education has an essential role in fostering our educational aims, so it is very important that the co-ordinator enthusiastically supports the concept of social education as a process and not just a concern with social facts and insights no matter how interesting those may be.

2. Applicants will need to show not only their own faith in this notion of social education, but also an ability to convince other colleagues of the worth of this work.

3. The successful applicant will work with other senior colleagues—both heads of year who play a major part in social education, and heads of faculty and department who contribute both to the specific social education programme and the social education content of the wider curriculum. This will call for tact and diplomacy, and strong leadership. The ability to sustain belief in the worth of social education even in times of self-doubt and opposition, and the ability to inspire other colleagues would be very helpful attributes.

4. The co-ordinator will not be working alone. The senior management are fully committed to social education. The present deputy head (curriculum) was the previous co-ordinator. The majority of staff are involved either in the timetabled social education, or in the pastoral curriculum. Further, the main innovatory work has been completed over the six years during which the programme has been running. Consolidation and maintenance and improvement of effectiveness are now looked for.

5. Expertise in some of the following areas would be valued: Health education—moral education—sex education and education in personal relationships—politics—study skills—tutorial work—counselling—values—aesthetics—use of drama—religious education.

Role

1. The co-ordinator's role is a difficult one. There is no defined department of social education. Rather this is a job ranging across the curriculum, drawing skills, expertise and knowledge from most of the staff in the various subject areas.

2. The co-ordinator will organize a complex programme throughout the five years of the school. He/she will be responsible to the headmaster for aims, objectives, planning, content, learning resources, ordering, records, evaluation, and teaching techniques in the programme.

3. Even though the co-ordinator may not teach in all five years, he/she will still oversee these programmes. The heads of year may run their year programme with form tutors, but the co-ordinator will service the course and liaise with the heads of year.

4. In years 4–5 there is a modular course, which will be organized according to the needs of the pupils, and with the staff available in mind.

5. The co-ordinator liaises with the deputy head (pastoral) and the heads of year about the pastoral curriculum form periods, and will work closely with the deputy head (curriculum) and heads of faculty/departments to keep within view all the social education taking place in the school. Overlap an duplication of work need to be monitored.

6. We would expect the successful applicant to be alive to the teaching materials available in the social education area, to take an interest in curriculum development, to continue to develop our own teaching and learning materials through our resou centre, and to help colleagues reflec on their own practice.

7. There is a considerable pool of sk experience, and good will in the sch about social education which the n co-ordinator will use and develop.

eaching, but are ill at ease in the less ormal and more open-ended style of eaching which some aspects of this vork demand.

If we ask colleagues to take on this ind of work they may need new kills—which raises the need for urther professional training. There re local education authorities who rganize their own courses in astoral care, education in personal elationships, health, careers and llied areas of the curriculum. There re short courses run by the Aarriage Guidance Council, the amily Planning Association, the eachers' Advisory Centre for lcohol and Drug Education. There re full-time and part-time Diploma nd Advanced Diploma courses run y colleges of higher education and le institutes or departments of ducation of various universities, hich equip the teacher for this vork. Perhaps the greatest impact is 1ade by schools organizing their wn professional development ourses internally with the help of utside bodies.

The question of 'What?' has ready been discussed in the chapter 1 content. Practical organization is eeded to decide what topics, skills, 1d concepts to include at particular ges. Which subjects will contribute? here is need for *consultation* and *co- -dination*. It is quite wrong for a oup of teachers to put a topic into new course without consultation ith other interested parties. The ntent needs careful planning and -ordination, both in decisions out what topics the course may nsist of, and in the purchase, hire production of learning materials ch as books, curriculum packages

or kits, video tapes, films, booklets and worksheets. The syllabus or list of content needs developing into class-room learning experiences. Someone in the school should have an over-all picture of what is being taught and what is being learned in this dimension of the curriculum. How does this relate to the work of other subjects and to the over-all aims and values of the school? For this task a school needs to choose a fairly senior and well-respected member of staff. By way of illustration, the job description of a co-ordinator sent to applicants for the post at Rotheram High School is reproduced opposite.

Closely linked to the co-ordinating of this work are the questions of 'When?' and 'Where?' The allocation of time, resources, timetabling and rooming are important factors. Personal, Social and Moral Education needs someone to argue the case for these organizational concerns, and who will plan and translate these factors into effective action. There needs to be a good head of department. Whatever method of timetabling or organization is adopted, a school needs an adequate amount of capitation, staffing and suitable accommodation, just as for any other subject. Decisions will need to be made about how to group the pupils. I personally favour mixed-ability groups. *All* our pupils take this 'Social Education', as we call it. A co-ordinator will need time to prepare new learning materials, space for housing them, and secretarial assistance in typing and reprographics.

A lot more could be said about

organization, but in summary I offer the following points for consideration:

● The organization of this work is likely to flounder and be ineffective where there is:
—inadequate preparatory planning and consultation
—inadequate support from senior staff
—inadequate resources of timetabled time, finance, and staff with appropriate skills.

● Personal, Social and Moral Education is more likely to be effective when a person of vision, energy and diplomacy is appointed as a co-ordinator of this aspect of the curriculum.

● To be successful a co-ordinator needs power, authority and status from the senior management, and the respect of colleagues.

● Schemes can wither and die through lack of leadership, unwillingness to experiment and learn, resistance to change, and lack of will to solve problems and negotiate difficulties.

● Although there is great value in single subjects or individual teachers contributing to this aspect of pupils' education, there is likely to be a greater impact where a whole curriculum approach is worked out, particularly where the aims of the Personal, Social and Moral Education programme are matched by the values of the school and its actual practice.

Footnote

1. K. David, *Personal and Social Education in Secondary Schools*.

CHAPTER 8

WHAT HAPPENS IN THE CLASS-ROOM

Teachers are naturally suspicious of theory unless it relates directly to the practical task of teaching, or to the learning and behaviour of the pupils. Before we look at methods in detail, I want to propose seven practical principles about teaching and learning in Personal, Social and Moral Education. There is nothing original here. Practising teachers will immediately recognize the importance of at least some of them:

● Our teaching, and the learning tasks should spring from *pupil interests*, or at the very least have *direct relevance* to their present or future lives.

● As far as possible the teaching and learning processes should demand or involve as much *pupil participation* as possible.

● The teacher should cultivate warm, accepting and trusting *teacher/pupil* and *pupil/pupil relationships*.

● There should be *clarity of aims and purposes* in what we do in the class-room.

● The activities given to pupils in the classroom should have *real demand in learning*.

● Teachers should be harnessing both their own and the pupils' *imagination in the learning task* set.

● There should be *ongoing appraisal, review and evaluation* by the pupils as well as the teacher.

I have summarized for the sake of conciseness. But a few supporting and explanatory statements may be of help. I have already discussed pupil-interest in chapter 2, under the psychological justifications for this work. I find I cannot get very far in the class-room unless the topic or the skills I am teaching touch the pupils at the centre of their person. There is a sense in which we need the acquiescence of our pupils in this area of the curriculum. They will not

learn much if they are not willing—if they are saying, 'It's boring', or, 'I can't see the point of that.' Further, we need pupils taking an active part in these lessons. We do not want them to be passive receivers of lists of facts or bodies of knowledge. We want them to be more involved in the *process* than the content. I want them working things out for themselves, making the knowledge their own, clarifying their ideas, beliefs and values, learning and practising skills, and reflecting on their own behaviour. As the old proverb puts it: 'I hear and I forget. I see and I remember. I do and I understand.'

The relationship between the teacher and pupils is vital if social or moral learning is to take place. Children enduring teachers they neither like nor respect are unlikely to learn or to be receptive to lessons about personal, moral or social issues. A teacher needs to work at creating an accepting, trusting and warm climate in the class-room. Lesley Button has much to say about this in *Group Tutoring for the Form Teacher*. We need to think hard how our teaching style, the arrangement of class-room furniture, our attitude to children, our interaction with them outside the class-room, need adjusting to build the kind of relationships and atmosphere which helps pupils to learn.

We are not entertainers, or purveyors of 'deeply meaningful experiences'. There needs to be real demand in learning from these class-room experiences. Our aim is not 'to have a discussion', but to have a 'purposeful discussion' in order that we may learn something. We do not exchange ideas for the fun of it, see films to savour the emotional reactions of the characters, or have group quasi-mystical therapy to

wallow in our own consciousness. Reflection about ourselves is for personal growth. Group experiences are to help us learn about relationships. Emotional stimuli in the class-room are purposeful. Discussion is to explore points of view, to aid understanding, to clarify ideas. I am suspicious of sloppy thinking and uneducative activities in this field of education.

I am very keen on imagination in the class-room. Of course we should use the well-tried and trusted teaching techniques that we feel comfortable with, but we can use our imagination a lot more in what we do. Lessons should not be mundane and dull all the time. We are all conscious of some failings in this area! This is where I find it helps to review and evaluate what I have been doing with my classes. I encourage the painful but fruitful practice of allowing the children to write about what they like and dislike about the lessons, what they have learned, how the lessons could be improved, and how the lessons have helped them. These seven principles are a kind of mental check-list which help me review the work in the class-room.

There are, of course, many possible approaches and techniques to our work in the class-room. I have arranged these in the chart opposite from the most closed to the most open, from those where the learner has least control to those where he/she has most control in learning.

Doubtless the reader can think of other approaches. But first let me make my meaning clear.

Conditioning is where the teacher deliberately sets out to influence the learners' thinking or behaviour in a particular way without their consent or even knowledge. This is covert, manipulative and limits the freedom of the learner. McPhail discusses

. F. Skinner's behaviouristic views
f morality in *Social and Moral
ducation*.[1] Teachers do condition
upils by rewards and punishment.
his raises many questions about the
orality of conditioning, and
hether it is an educational process
all. *Indoctrination* is another bogey
ord in education. Undoubtedly
any schools try to indoctrinate their
upils, that is, they try to get them
accept a particular set of values or
eliefs, or to behave in a particular
ay. Indoctrination is the
ropagation of a particular view
ithout the learner having freedom
use his mind to consider
ternatives and decide for himself.
e indoctrinate children into
cceptable behaviour', into the
alues of our schools, and sometimes
to religious beliefs. The reader will
ecide to what extent these two
pproaches are legitimate in
ersonal, Social and Moral
ducation.

Instruction and training methods
e familiar to teachers, part of our
sic stock of skills, especially when
e want to teach bodies of
nowledge and particular skills. We
n instruct children in the laws
pplying to cyclists on our roads, and
e can train them in how to use
eir bicycles safely. There may be
irly low levels of understanding,
ch as recognition, recall, imitative
simple apprentice copying. With
planation or insight there may be
gher levels of learning which
volve reconstructive understanding,
awareness of the reasons and
urposes in the learning. Chalk and

Conditioning	**CLOSED**
Indoctrination	
Instruction/training	
Confrontation/exhortation	
Rational argument/persuasion	
Guided discussion	
Oblique experiential or inductive	
ethods	
Empathy methods	
Training in moral reasoning and	
oral dilemmas	
Values clarification strategies	
Procedural neutrality	
Non-directive group work or	
unselling	
Laissez-faire	**OPEN**

talk, memory tests, demonstrations
and practice are simple training and
instruction methods. The ability to
apply such knowledge or skills in
other situations, to solve problems,
to make inferences, judgements,
evaluations and to be creative are
often levels of learning that
straightforward instruction and
training do not develop. In the
matrix of personal, social and moral
development there are dimensions
where we want higher or other
dimensions of learning which
demand different strategies and
skills. We may train children in
social skills. One example might be
how to present themselves effectively
at an interview. The pupil may learn
five key points for success, in the
sense of being able to recall them,
but if he cannot apply them at his
interview the learning has been
inadequate. It will be much more
likely to have a lasting effect on the
children if we use imagination and
principles of participation, for
instance in role play and simulated
interviews where, say, four pupils are
interviewed by other children, or
local industrialists or trades-people.
The class is then given the chance to
discuss the skills and performance of
the pupils.

Instruction and training are very
important in teaching our children
how to behave. But children are
notoriously independent!
Confrontation, saying how you see it,
'telling it the way it is', is often
necessary to stop a wilful child
taking other pupils' pens in a
changing-room, or bullying in the
playground. *Rational argument and
persuasion* about racism is often
unable to overcome ingrained
prejudice. But if we can get a child
to see how it feels to be in another's
shoes, this may have a greater
learning impact. Drama, theatre,
films, videos, literature, BBC Schools
Broadcasts such as 'Scene', or poems
such as Adrian Mitchell's 'The
Killing Ground', can be used to help
the pupil enter imaginatively into the
experience of others. Children can
learn through the emotional impact
of the stimulus, by identifying with
the characters in the novel, by feeling
how it is to be treated in a particular
way. As I have mentioned before,

McPhail[2] has developed several
learning packages based on cards
depicting social situations. These are
designed to arouse this kind of
awareness of other people, this skill
and response of *empathy*.

When I am trying to give children
fresh insights or a different slant on a
personal situation, a moral problem,
or a social evil, I sometimes find that
they are locked into attitudes and
will not open their minds to other
possibilities. Instruction, training,
argument, discussion, and even
empathy techniques all appear
counter-productive. But it is
sometimes possible to use what I call
oblique experiential methods or
inductive processes. An example of
this would be where children are
using the word 'spastic' against any
child who has a handicap or minor
disfigurement. Other approaches and
techniques appear to have failed. A
visit to a local children's hospital for
the mentally handicapped is arranged
for these name-callers, with consent
from their parents. The children go
and experience the problems of the
mentally handicapped—and some
come back with a different view of
spastics. They have learned because
they have been physically and
emotionally involved in others'
problems. Compassion has been
aroused and behaviour changes. It
does not always work, of course, but
if we can give children real, live
experiences of what we are teaching,
the total impact for learning is
greater.

This applies to another important
skill we need to develop: *inductive
teaching*. This is the art of using the
real experience of boys and girls,
harnessing their feelings, the
happenings in their lives. The
greatest resource we have is the
experience and consciousness that the
children bring with them into our
class-room. We can do this by
allowing them to write about
themselves, their attitudes, their
feelings, ambitions and hopes, fears,
beliefs. *Values Clarification* strategies
mentioned in chapter 3 are very
helpful. I encourage classes to keep
values journals, where they can think
and reflect, comment and describe
experiences, write about
relationships, try out new ideas,

consider alternative views on controversial issues. These are confidential, the property of the student. I will never look at them unless invited, and will not press the owner to reveal anything he or she does not wish to make known.

We need *group work skills* for this work. We can read about it, but I believe the only way to learn effectively is to experience these skills by joining a course in group skills. Various universities, organizations and local education authorities run such courses. The role of the teacher changes from instructor and imparter of information to *facilitator*. Silences need to be endured, minority opinions protected, dominant views probed, thinking clarified, alternative views considered, all contributions accepted (whether or not we happen to agree with them), feelings explored, consequences of behaviour considered.

There are implications for class-room organization: desks need to be moved about; children may sit in circles instead of rows; talking may become the norm, rather than writing and listening; the physical structure of the class-room may need changing. For example, I found group work more successful in a sixth-form block which had carpeted floors and easy chairs in small tutorial rooms, than in formal class-rooms. The relationship between teacher and pupil will certainly change: it will become less formal and less authoritarian; it will become more accepting, warm and sharing; social distance diminishes; the teacher becomes willing to open up his feelings and attitudes and is willing to expose more private aspects of his personality than perhaps he had previously shared in formal class-rooms.

There are a variety of approaches to group work. Sheila Thompson and J. H. Kahn's *The Group Process as a Helping Technique*[3] is a useful introduction. So too is the writing of Lesley Button, already mentioned. The guides to the Humanities Curriculum Project—particularly the work of Lawrence Stenhouse—is essential reading.[4]

Are all these changes in the traditional role of the teacher necessary? Can we use the didactic, instructional, expository styles we are familiar with? I am sure there is a lot of room for teaching in the way we feel most secure, but we do need *appropriate* teaching strategies for particular aims, purposes and processes. Instructional, expository styles can be very effective in assemblies. Great preachers, as I know at first-hand, have enormous impact on the understanding of their congregations. We all need to equip ourselves with appropriate strategies and skills. If we want to engage in discussion, we must learn the skills of breaking the class up into small groups, twos or threes. Aims which demand deeper levels of understanding may require us to learn skills in role play or in dealing with groups. If we want powerful stimuli to learning in the class-room we must master the *educational technology*: tape-recorders, filmstrip and 16mm projectors, video machines, cameras. If we want children to learn about morality, moral decisions and thinking, we must equip ourselves with the skills involved in case studies, moral dilemmas, and perhaps procedural neutrality where human issues are controversial. The kinds of learning in Personal, Social and Moral Education are more demanding for the student and more demanding for the teacher. This is why the principles established at the beginning of this chapter are so important. There is little value in a *laissez-faire* attitude: 'The children will learn something, whatever I do.' Education needs to be planned. Of course, a lot is learned incidentally. There are unintended consequences, some positive, and some negative. Attitudes can become hardened, prejudices reinforced, if pupils have complete freedom and control over their learning. They do need to be fully involved, their minds active, interest aroused, experience valued, opinions accepted and emotions aroused—and to do this we need a wide range of alternative approaches, teaching skills and strategies.

It is a lot easier actually to demonstrate these teaching strategies with a group of teachers than it is to talk or write about them. I participated in an Upper School Conference in Bedford recently, spending thirty minutes talking about this area of school life, followed by an hour and ten minute practical session on possible teaching strategies for tutorial work. I demonstrated simple techniques for discussion and games, using the staff as my class. The reaction of the staff was much more animated in the practical session, and comments afterwards confirmed that practical demonstration is much more effective than talk! I cannot arrange a practical demonstration in this book, but I have taken a number of photographs to illustrate my points.

There is a whole range of strategies that imaginative teachers employ, as well as the tried and tested methods of instruction we are all familiar with. I have no doubt that readers will know of many more but here are some we use at my school:

● *Individual work*. This includes writing, comprehension, worksheets, research, library work, surveys, creative writing, report writing, unfinished sentences, writing replies to problem letters, writing to newspapers, writing to organizations helping people, collages, exhibitions, word response tests, attitudes, beliefs and values clarified in a journal, cartoon work, drawing. Individual work has much merit, not just as a control mechanism but, more importantly, for helping children to sort out their thoughts. It also helps them form their own ideas, evaluations and opinions without the pressure of a group. In some schools learning seems to eddy around a swirl of worksheets. It is difficult to compose effective worksheets which are well designed, clear, appropriate in readability, and at the same time demanding of real learning from the pupils. It is quite common, when one visits schools, to be greeted by aerodynamic worksheets from the fourth floor! One look at them, and is easy to see why origami rules, rather than the teacher's methods! But well-designed, thoughtful worksheets can be an effective learning tool.

● *Dyads and triads.* Many teachers persist in trying to conduct whole-class discussions. No doubt many of these are excellent, but often a few pupils dominate the interchange of ideas. Breaking the class into pairs and threes can facilitate greater participation. Exchanging ideas, exploring meanings, problem-solving, reflection about different ideas, attitudes and beliefs, research—all manner of learning tasks may be set to pairs. Not only is there more participation, but shy or reticent pupils have opportunities to contribute away from public scrutiny. One game I particularly like is getting a pair to exchange views and then asking them to repeat the view of the partner to a third person. The original opinion-holders then tell each other how accurately they have listened and reported. There are many interpersonal relationship games that can be played in pairs and threes. We can start with something safe, like sharing favourite television programmes, and then graduate to the more personal, deeper levels: happiness, sadness, fear, ambitions, beliefs and so on. Lewis and Streitfeld's book and Lesley Button's work mentioned earlier have helpful suggestions. Dyad and triad work is useful for training in communication skills; listening, reporting, confidence boosting in oral expression and formulating ideas; it is useful in building self-awareness and self-esteem, in education for getting on with people, in promoting tolerance of differences, as well as the more usual sharing of answers on closed questions and blackboard comprehension exercises.

● *Small-group work.* Groups of four to six break up whole classes but demand more co-operation, more complex interaction than pairs. They generate a greater divergence of opinion, or pressure to conformity. Social skills training is effective in small groups: learning about non-verbal communication, eye movement, tone of voice; learning to listen, to negotiate, to be independent, to co-operate, to compromise for the sake of the majority, to make group decisions, to understand how others perceive us— the list is endless. Small-group work changes the authority structure in the class-room. The teacher's traditional 'purveyor of knowledge' role changes to facilitator, encourager, and consultant. The pupils have more power over their learning. Control is more difficult. However, teachers have little to fear, and much to gain in terms of social learning, commitment and motivation, understanding and interest in their pupils. The list of possible activities in groups is endless: discussion, organizing events, learning to take collective decisions, meeting procedures, role play, acting, simulations and games, taking photographs, mounting displays or exhibitions, observing the behaviour of other pupils, solving problems, reporting and representing others' views, conducting surveys, analysing newspapers, meeting people, making introductions. I find that problem-centred learning tasks for groups and games which involve diplomacy and negotiation with other groups are very effective. Case studies on a given topic—sexual behaviour, crime, family matters, abortion, racism—I have found to be a very helpful

SOURCES FOR TECHNIQUES

● Peter McPhail, *Social and Moral Education*, particularly chapter eight.
● J. Baldwin and H. Wells, *Active Tutorial Work*, is particularly rich in the 'how to' ways of organizing the work and in teaching strategies, as well as content. (These first two books are essential reading, a must for the bookshelf.)
● The Teachers' Guides to Projects such as *Lifeline*, *Think Well*, Health Education 5–13 and 13–18 are a rich source of ideas for teachers on methods in the class-room.
● The Teachers' Guide to the Schools Council Careers Education and Guidance Project: Work, Part 2, is extremely valuable. It describes how to go about the lessons it suggests. I wish more teachers would read and follow these guides. They are full of suggestions, detailed help, and even tell us just what to do! Where teachers adapt these ideas to their own teaching styles, instead of experimenting and learning new methods, their lessons are the poorer. I am using the 'Work Guide' with my fifteen-year-old careers group at present. I find it helpful, full of ideas for my busy schedule.
● Lesley Button, *Group Tutoring*, contains a lot of valuable help on games, group techniques, and activities for the children.
● Sidney Simon, *Meeting Yourself Halfway*, contains ideas for strategies and games for pupils and will inspire your own ideas.
● Paul Phillips and Franklin Cordell, *Am I OK?*, gives ideas to build on.
● Donna Brandes and Howard Phillips, *Gamesters' Handbook*, is useful for exercises, strategies and games for class-room, youth club or party.
● H. Lewis and H. Streitfeld, *Growth Games*, needs reading wisely, but has guidance for those wishing to devise their own original activities in class-rooms.
● Douglas Hamblin's books on *Pastoral Care, Counselling* and *Study Skills* are essential purchases for every secondary school staff-room.
● Educational television and schools broadcasts offer guidance on how to use the programmes, if teachers are patient in reading the small print. ITV produces 'Making a Living', 'Starting Out', and the BBC produces 'Scene', 'Good Job Prospects' and 'Going to Work'. These are just a few examples of the many programmes available, from sex education to politics.
● The time sacrificed reading the small print of the guides to curriculum packages, kits, films and books for class-room use is bountifully rewarded with ideas for teaching method and strategy. It is worth looking back at some of the older materials such as HCP, the Childwall Project, the Social Education Kits produced by MacMillan, to read the excellent suggestions about teaching method. More recent publications often explain in detail how to use the materials, but many teachers find neither the time nor the patience to read it. This is a pity because quite often they have been extensively tested by ordinary teachers.

method of getting a group to explore an issue, a question, a topic, at some depth. It distances them from the privacy of their feelings on the topic and gives them skills in solving human problems by considering alternatives and consequences. If they want to, they can relate their own experiences to a group, to gain support or help, or more privately relate the case study to their own situation. A lot of counselling arises from topical case studies about other teenagers. Real cases, with confidentiality protected by changing identifiable details, are more effective than fictitious ones. The 'truth' element is important to many pupils. Some do not like 'just playing games, sir'. Moral dilemmas of the type Kolberg has introduced are excellent motivators for thinking about moral problems. My groups feel very 'let down' if I do not use true cases. Scanning newspapers yields material for moral dilemmas.

Children need training in how to co-operate and work in groups. If chaos ensues at first in classes unfamiliar with group work, the teacher must persist and train the class—good work will follow. Nominal Group Technique is a good training strategy. It involves writing in silence, followed by pupils reading their opinions aloud in turn. The teacher notes them on a board. Each participant is protected from comments, interruptions or abuse. There is no discussion at first. When each member of the group has had a turn, the teacher goes 'round-robin' again. When the time allocated is up, or opinions are exhausted, there is a time for questions about the comments on the board. Next, the pupils choose five of the opinions on the board, and score them 1–5 in ascending order of importance. The teacher can make a score tally at the end for the consensus view. Discussion follows.[5] Larger groups of 12–16 pupils need the special

groups skills mentioned earlier. Teachers would be unwise to embark on developmental group work without some training.

● *Whole class work*. Experienced teachers need little comment on this. I recommend the impact and stimulus of audio-visual programmes such as those produced by Mary Glasgow, by the educational television producers, and other commercial producers mentioned in the appendix. Some excellent sound tapes are also available of various situations for discussion, writing and other class-room activities. There are many insights that we cannot teach or instruct. If we can provide rich and dynamic experiences about personal, social and moral life, maybe the pupils will have the chance of responding to these stimuli and gain insights which are difficult to teach.

Whatever size of group, or particular teaching strategy we adopt, the attitude of the pupils to their learning is vital. We all know that teaching teenagers is difficult. There are problems of motivation. We have to deal with distracting interests and preoccupations in the pupil, overcome prejudice against the subject, pupils' dislike of the teacher, tension between groups of children, and dislike of the particular topic. I do not believe we should accommodate our teaching to every teenage whim and mood, but I have found that it is important to work to create friendly, warm, accepting working relationships with the pupils. If there is little respect, if there is little affection in the attitude of the pupil to the teacher, in my experience little is learnt in Personal, Social and Moral Education. Acceptance of the teacher's personality appears to be an important step in the pupil's acceptance of the content and process of these lessons. Time spent in

organizing visits, school trips, sports and games, and friendly chats in the corridor, is generously rewarded with better relationships in the class-room and more learning. Time spent camping, or at the theatre, on residentials or organizing clubs, is teaching capital wisely invested.

Working in this area can be discouraging and frustrating. We wonder if there is any impact. We cannot see the outcome of our work very clearly. There is a time-lag, the 'sleeper effect'. We cannot know immediately if young people will actually practise the skills we have tried to teach: to help them cope with employment, parenthood, relationships, or moral decisions. We may observe heightened awareness, greater sensitivity, changes in behaviour or increased understanding of particular issues. But we cannot know whether this learning will last. Years later children, by then grown-up, will come back (hopefully) and reassure us that it was all worthwhile! Faith and hope are important qualities for teachers in this area of the curriculum where learning outcomes are not neatly measurable and open to the same kind of assessment as in other areas of the curriculum. Despite all the difficulties, however, it remains vitally important.

Footnotes

1. P. McPhail, *Social and Moral Education*.
2. P. McPhail, *Lifeline*, 'How Are We Feeling Today?'
3. Sheila Thompson, J. H. Kahn, *The Group Process as a Helping Technique*
4. 'Controversial values issues in the class-room', in W. G. Carr, *Values and the Curriculum*.
5. Readers interested in this technique can consult B. S. Collinson and S. F. Dunlap, *School Counsellor*, Vol. 26, No. 1, 1978.

CHAPTER 9

ASSESSMENT AND EVALUATION

The ideas of assessment and evaluation cause apprehension and disquiet in student and teacher alike. As I write, pupils have been waiting anxiously for their GCE 'O' level results, and teachers have been reading in the educational press more about 'accountability' and 'appraisals'. This is a sensitive area, yet it is most important that teachers and their pupils reflect about what they have been learning. But what do I mean by assessment and evaluation?

By 'assessment' I mean the process of determining what a pupil has learned, noting a student's level of performance in relation to a particular educational aim or process. It may be the recall of factual knowledge, the understanding of concepts, the grasp of mental processes, the attitudes, dispositions and values of the learner, or it may be the practical application of skills, habits, beliefs or behaviour.

'Evaluation' is the description and the gathering of information about the effects and value of educational activities. The observation of learning and teaching in schools, with careful recording and analysis, is the process of evaluation. Judgements about the worth of these activities may be made by the teachers involved, with a view to improvement. This is sometimes called 'formative evaluation'. 'Summative evaluation' is a phrase used to describe the judgement of the worth of a programme at its completion. These judgements may be made by inspectors, administrators or politicians.

Of course, there is nothing new about teachers assessing the work of their pupils. We have asked questions in class to determine understanding. We have devised tests of various kinds which purport to record how much our pupils have learned. We mark written work and assess practical exercises—out of ten, as a percentage, with letters A to E, or by awarding other symbols. These marks may be a nightmare to the statistician, and of dubious validity but we all recognize these forms of assessment! The external examinations, grades, pass marks, continuous assessment, and projects are all part of the pupil's vocabulary. David Slatterly has written a very helpful volume for teachers who, like me, find statistics difficult.[1] He surveys a technical area including standardized tests, teacher-made tests, rating scales and check-lists, giving practical help in the use of assessment techniques and their value.

In the area of Personal, Social and Moral Education, the Assessment and Performance Unit of the Department of Education and Science came across particular difficulties in trying to assess pupil performance: 'It was recognized that the Unit was here moving into a sensitive and controversial area, and that proposals to monitor children's development in such matters as moral or religious attitudes might well be regarded as an undesirable encroachment upon privacy and the rights of the individual . . . By 1980 . . . it was also apparent that there was no satisfactory way round the difficulties inherent in proposals for assessment in this area.'[2] They did, however, produce a survey of international literature which should be consulted by serious students.[3]

There are 'particular difficulties' in assessing our pupils in this area:

● Who is to decide what counts as the 'good' or 'right' moral or social qualities that we are to assess?

● Are there valid and effective instruments for observing or measuring these attributes?

● How do we defend ourselves against the charges of indoctrination or social engineering when we want to foster particular personal qualities?

● Can we be sure that our pupils display the same character traits in social situations outside the school?

● What are we attempting to measure, if indeed it can be measured?

Assessment in some disciplines is more straightforward. We can assess a pupil's understanding of 'standard deviation' or of the concept of 'density' by testing them in problems where that understanding must be demonstrated. But what of qualities such as 'truthfulness' or 'responsibility'? If a test is devised, whether written or practical, the candidate can generate the correct response for the test without having any intention of working that principle into his life. There are particular difficulties in the practical as well as ethical and political areas. Observations may be coloured by a teacher's view of the child in question. In other class-rooms pupils may behave or respond differently. Further, there is what Ken David calls the 'sleeper effect'. There may be little or no apparent effect for some time, but behaviour or attitude changes may appear later.

Should teachers eschew all ideas of assessment in Personal, Social and Moral Education because of the sensitivity of the area and the difficulties inherent in assessment? Standardized tests and attitudes scales may appear more objective than the teacher's 'gut reactions' but they can be difficult to devise and expensive to operate in terms both of time and finance. They are likely to have limited value for the busy teacher.

How, then, should teachers proceed? How do we give an account of pupils' learning in our school's Personal, Social and Moral Education? I believe we should be accountable both to parents and to authorities for the resources invested in this work. I want to suggest a number of practical ways forward:

● First, we need to state what we are trying to do, and why. Critics outside the school will blame the PSME programme for all sorts of failings it was never designed to tackle. If we are realistic in our aims, modest in our claims, it helps. We cannot change human personality, reverse trends in family life overnight, or blot out major ills in society with one thirty-minute period a week!

● Second, there are areas of PSME which are subject to the normal assessment procedures. We can, for instance, determine pupils' knowledge of the law as it affects young people, their understanding of human reproduction, their grasp of the beliefs of political parties, or of any topic where pupils are asked to recognize or recall information. These topics can be tested and assessed by question and answer techniques where there are closed right/wrong answers. If we are trying to teach children about road safety, we can test some aspects of their knowledge by, say, alternative-answer questions.

● Third, there is a lot we can do in the assessing of pupil performance in particular skills. Skills training in PSME has become popular recently. If we define the skill we are seeking to teach, we can set up a situation to test that skill. When I teach basketball skills such as shooting, dribbling or passing, I can set up a test in which the pupil must show the extent to which he has mastered the skill. We can do this with *communication skills:* listening, reporting, speaking in public, summarizing, chairing, and so on. We can do this with *social skills:* handling conflict, meeting new people, awareness of non-verbal signals, how to present yourself at an

interview, how to ask a girl for a date, how to dress for particular occasions, and so on. We can do this for *health skills* such as care of the teeth, personal hygiene, balanced meals, avoidance of harmful substances—although, of course, this area is more difficult because we cannot monitor the skills away from school. We can do this in *employment skills:* choosing an area of interest, self-assessment of abilities and aptitudes, applications for further education, employment and training schemes, and so on. Wherever these skills are used it may be possible to determine the criterion of achievement and to assess against that.

● Fourth, if we are teaching young people the skills of Values Clarification in a moral education programme, it would be possible to devise an assessment procedure on how effectively they demonstrated

these seven processes in the class-room. This could be done intuitively, impressionistically from teachers' notes, or by stating the criteria carefully about the choosing, prizing, affirming and acting on a four-point scale—and devising an instrument to test these processes. It is important to state the criteria, what it is the pupils have to do, otherwise our assessments can degenerate into guesswork.

Methods of assessing moral development in Kohlberg's terms are available. It is possible to categorize pupils' reasoning about moral dilemmas in relation to the stages of moral development. C. Power, at the University of Boston, devised a manual for coding and scoring statements made by students and teachers at community meetings in a 'just community' school, Cambridge Cluster School, Boston.[5] This school was set up to implement Kohlberg's five conditions for moral growth:[6]

ASSESSING SKILLS

There are many examples in 'Profile Reports for School Leavers' by Janet Balogh.[4]

A Simple *'can do' profiles:* ✓

| Can listen to get information | ☐ |

| Can talk to strangers | ☐ |

Can hold a conversation describing/giving information
                    asking questions
                  answering questions
               explaining something
      giving an opinion or evaluation

B More specific *'criteria' profiles:* ✓

Communication oral skills: | 1 | 2 | 3 | 4 |

Grade 1 = Can argue a point of view, or present a case. Consistently uses correct, fluent and appropriate expression. Has clear diction. Understands complex spoken ideas and instructions.

Grade 2 = Willing to express ideas or opinions, and speaks easily. Expression is not always appropriate. Diction can be slovenly. Appears to understand spoken instructions.

Grade 3 = Hesitates to speak out; but makes points adequately, though not easily, when pressed. Some marked weaknesses of expression and diction.

Grade 4 = Communication limited to simple messages and instructions. Speech poorly organized, often irrelevant and inaccurate. Diction poor.

(Source: Rotheram High School Computer Assessment Manual)

1. Exposure to cognitive moral conflict
2. Role taking
3. Consideration of fairness and morality
4. Exposure to the next stage of moral reasoning
5. Active participation in group decision-making

When we come to the deeper levels of understanding a topic or a discipline, to the principles, procedures, ways of solving problems, what counts as evidence, or to insights into human and moral situations, I am far less happy about the use of the word 'assess'. I prefer a *description in words* of a pupil's understanding, as far as we have been able to comprehend it. We may get glimpses of what a child understands about human problems, of their sensitivity to beauty or truth, through essays or in discussion. But we can never really be sure what is going on in their mind and spirit. We certainly cannot 'measure'. 'Assessment' is dubious. 'Description' of what we may have observed about their understanding would seem more appropriate.

The more we move *away* from questions of information, facts and skills, *towards* sensitive, moral and spiritual understanding, human issues and consciousness, the less 'measurement', 'assessment' and 'judgement' are appropriate. I am attracted to a form of profiling where student as well as teacher writes about personal qualities. If a school wishes to inculcate honesty, justice, co-operativeness, diligence, or any other quality, let the pupil take part in his own description of his qualities (and let the teachers think hard about their own personal qualities too!). It is possible to use the specific criteria four-point scale method or the 'tends towards' method of recording personal qualities.

I have found that if we teach young people to reflect about their own opinions, beliefs, attitudes and behaviour they will write about themselves with deep insight. I welcome the renewed interest, in Swindon's Record of Personal Achievement, of student profiling, and of pupils being taught to assess their own personality traits. Pupils

are very astute and surprisingly honest if we let them discuss their own leaving reports, and (dare I say it?) even contribute to their leaving profile of achievement.

Much of what we set out to do cannot be assessed easily. Preparation for life skills, training in parenthood, moral education, self-awareness—all have the 'sleeper effect'. We can only partially assess how far we have made our students politically literate,

or to what extent they have developed self-confidence. We do not know directly how their attitudes, beliefs and behaviour have been affected outside school, and in adult life. Occasionally parents may drop by and tell us. Or we may bump into old students who renew our resolve and belief that it is all worth while. We have to live with these uncertainties. The fact that much of our work is not measurable makes it

DECISION-MAKING SKILLS

← —————— TENDS TOWARDS —————— →

Can find information with guidance				Shows initiative in gathering information from a variety of sources
Can solve problems with guidance				Can supply alternative methods of problem-solving, and select best method
Can plan simple operations with guidance				Plans work thoroughly, considers all implications, and uses all available sources for help
Can cope with everyday problems with guidance				Can offer sensitive and effective help to other people facing problems

SELF-AWARENESS

Is aware of own personality and situation	—Grade 4
Can determine own strengths, weaknesses and preferences with guidance	—Grade 3
Has a good understanding of his own situation, personality and motivation	—Grade 2
Has a thorough understanding of own personality and abilities and their implication	—Grade 1

1	2	3	4

(Source: City and Guilds course 365 Vocational Preparation)

RELIABILITY

← —————— TENDS TOWARDS —————— →

Needs to work under firm supervision. Unwise to depend too heavily upon him/her.				Can be trusted to work alone. Will complete a job. Can be left in charge of others or expensive machinery with confidence.

no less worth while. Much more research is needed into ways of assessing PSME.

Evaluation is perhaps the more painful of the two processes for the teacher. However, there is nothing new about teachers reflecting on their own work, and making judgements about the effectiveness of materials, methods, and learning processes. Thoughtful teachers do this intuitively. We ask questions, review progress, try to improve what we are doing. We do not like other people peering through the window, making judgements about us from outside. Teaching is insecure enough without critical eyes gazing into class-rooms. However, I believe evaluation is here to stay for some time, particularly in view of calls for greater accountability and teacher-appraisals. It is in our own interest to be ready to give account of what we do. Many local authorities in England are producing check-lists for self-evaluation in schools, in the footsteps of the Inner London Education Committee's 'Keeping the School Under Review' (1977). Too few of these check-lists, it would seem, are concerned with class-room processes of teaching and learning. It is my hope that teachers reading this section will be encouraged to look more closely and systematically at PSME with a view to evaluating and improving what they are doing. This is the essence of 'action-research'.

The current state of evaluation in the UK is reflected in *Calling Education to Account*, an Open University set book.[7] I warmly recommend this book. *Studying Class-rooms*[8] is an excellent guide to practical methods for teachers evaluating their own class-room work. These books are particularly helpful. Evaluating our work is not straightforward.

I have tomatoes growing in my conservatory. If I control the growing environment, the temperature, soil, the watering and feeding, I can be hopeful of good fruit. The right conditions produce growth. Learning and teaching are more complex. So too is the social reality of the class-room. There are more variables. Motivation, relationships with the teacher, peer

pressures, pupil expectations of the teacher, the school ethos, the status of the lesson—all these play a part, as well as teaching method, appropriate materials and learning processes. There is a mystery in teaching children. You can teach a lesson to one group, and they race ahead with their understanding. Yet an identical lesson with another group fails to break through the yawning boredom! How, then, are we to evaluate our work? What practical steps may we take?

● We can continue the intuitive, semi-automatic reflection and appraisal which is part of everday practice. We can ask ourselves: How did the lesson go? Why were they looking puzzled? How can I try to make this clearer? What is the best way to motivate and capture interest? How can I put over that idea more clearly? What was it I was actually trying to teach? What did I ask them to do? Were the kids just thick today, or was it me? What did they actually learn?

● We can help each other evaluate our work by discussion, sharing ideas, and deliberation with colleagues. This, too, is part of school life: departmental meetings, case conferences for pastoral staff, in-service sessions where common interests or problems are discussed, staff meetings large or small which are genuinely exploratory, with thought-provoking exchanges about real class-room teaching and learning problems and interests, and not just information-giving or sermonizing by the headteacher.

Since we introduced departmental meetings into our school timetable this deliberation, collaborative appraisal and review of teaching materials, consideration of alternative methods and improvement of the quality of learning has begun to flourish. This is particularly important in an area of innovation, or where we are co-operating with other teachers or departments in a big school. PSME needs this collaborative, consultative forum for evaluation.

● There are tools of evaluation that we can acquire by reading, experimentation and practice. Groups of teachers through the Open

University courses and in various national projects such as Ford Teaching Project, and the Schools Council Teacher-Pupil Interaction and the Quality of Learning Project have acquired some of these action-research skills. Action-research is the 'systematic reflection on practical problems experienced by teachers with a view to arriving at some decision about what ought to be done about them'.[9] Teachers use the skills and insights derived from Social Science, Anthropology, and various approaches to educational evaluation. If all this sounds rather technical let me give some practical examples of what can be done.

Likert surveys

I wanted to find out whether the attitudes of some 16 year-old pupils was really as negative as it appeared to me in newly-introduced PSME lessons. I devised the series of statements about the work, reproduced opposite, and asked the pupils to respond with a tick where it expressed their opinion or attitude.

I tried to cover the areas I was interested in. I put in check questions such as interesting/boring, and about the purposes of education, to see if pupils were filling in the responses indiscriminately.

I did not make a statistical analysis, but derived some general conclusions about the main drift of attitudes. I was pleasantly surprised by the amount of positive feeling. In the surveys, the few vocal critics in class were outweighed by the more reticent majorities.

Unfinished sentence techniques

Later in our work we wanted to see what attitudes our 15-year-old pupils had to PSME:
● What they liked about the course.
● What they disliked.
● What they found most helpful.
● I wanted to discover if they could state why we had PSME, and to compare their perceptions with my aims.
● I wanted to see if pupils could recount any specific outcomes of the course or things they had learned.

I used these simple unfinished sentences:

   a. I like PSME because . . .
   b. I dislike PSME because . . .
   c. The most helpful thing was . . .
   d. I think we have PSME because . . .

Unfinished sentences provide a rich source of pupil-ideas. Due care must be taken to limit bias and to ensure truthfulness. We found much to encourage, much to adjust and much to improve for the next year. This simple technique elicits pupil responses on a wide variety of evaluation topics. For example, Moral Education:

   In these lessons I have learned . . .
   I could not do this before but I can now . . .
   The way that I have changed is . . .
   The most important thing about 'X' is . . .
   My thinking about 'X' has changed because . . .

The reliability of this data, and the validity of conclusions drawn from it can be problematic if we do not try to ensure truthfulness. I make the responses anonymous, and build in balances and checks. A useful check is using further pupil-writing, or asking a colleague to interview a few of the pupils. I have allowed the press, educational researchers, BBC Radio and TV, and ITV reporters to interview the children. This is always risky! You never know what they might say in front of outsiders. However, it does indicate in surprising ways what they are learning. Recently a group was interviewed by a visitor. From the report I heard, they said that they did not carry over much of what they learned in the class-room to their lives outside. Then one girl unconsciously demonstrated how she had learned to role-take, to put herself in someone else's shoes. She said, 'You ask those that have left. I think they'll tell you that it is helpful, though you don't know it at the time.'

Interviews

Free-wheeling or structured questioning in interviews yields a lot of information about children's learning. I have interviewed pupils for other colleagues, and they have interviewed pupils of mine. Interviews can probe understanding, find out the pupil's view of the learning and teaching. They can check the reliability of data, too, for the exaggeration, group pressure statements, reasons for quietness in class—all these can be probed more deeply. These interviews can also teach us a lot about our own

PUPIL RESPONSE	Strongly agree	Agree	Undecided	Disagree	Strongly disagree
1. I have found PSME interesting					
2. PSME is a waste of time because it does not help us					
3. PSME should lead to an exam					
4. I learned a lot in the fourth-year course					
5. We need to be taught about politics					
6. I have found PSME boring					
7. We need PSME to prepare us for life outside school					
8. The opportunity to discuss topics makes an interesting break from exam subjects					
9. The main purpose of education is to get a job					
10. We need to know about the environment					
11. The most enjoyable writing subject is English					
12. School should give young people help on growing up, love, sex, marriage					
13. Too much time was spent on writing					
14. School is a training-ground for adult life					
15. PSME time would more usefully be spent on examination subjects					
16. Too much time in PSME was spent talking and listening					
17. Too much time is spent in school doing exam work					
18. Community Service is valuable experience for fifth-year pupils					
19. Films in PSME have been helpful in learning					
20. Too much time was spent sitting in the class-room.					

organization, language and methodology in the class-room.

Tape recorders, video and radio microphones

These can be useful tools in our evaluation work. A simple tape-recording of teacher-talk can reveal complex language patterns, or difficult concepts lurking behind deceptively easy language. We make use of recorders, play back the cassette and transcribe the talk where appropriate. Analysis of the interaction between pupil and teacher can show a great deal—about teaching method, questioning techniques, which children are participating, and many other features of class-room life.

Photographs, slides, and video tapes have the added advantage that the teacher can study his or her own practice visually. The first time I saw a video of my own teaching was quite an eye-opener. I became aware of certain aspects of my own teaching for the first time.

Triangulation

Triangulation 'involves gathering accounts of a teaching situation from three quite different points of view: those of the teacher, the students, and a participant observer'.[10]
If we are interested in the moral development of pupils and plan a lesson with a Kohlberg-type dilemma, we could use triangulation to look at the learning from three different viewpoints. The teacher explains to the observer what he hopes to do, what his aims are. The observer unobtrusively watches the process of teaching and learning, making his own field notes. At the end of the lesson the observer negotiates with teacher and pupils to interview a small group of pupils about their perception of what the lesson was all about, what they were learning, what they found hard to understand. This may be recorded. The teacher talks to the observer about his lesson. Then the three separate accounts of observer, pupils and teacher are compared. Theories about what was going on can be tested against the other views.

I have found triangulation a very helpful and productive method of

giving insights into the teaching and learning process. The teacher critically examines his own practice. He may feel exposed, but the insights gained are worth the temporary embarrassment. I have found that the pupils, rather than take advantage of the teacher, show an increased interest in their own learning. Triangulation seems to increase student motivation, as well as help the teacher evaluate his work.[11]

Other methods

There are a whole host of other methods: check-lists, observational instruments, behaviour sampling methods, questionnaires, inventories, sociometric methods and case study methods. Space prevents me mentioning them. I leave the psychometric tests for others better qualified to comment upon. My own preference is for the illuminative, social/anthropological paradigm of evaluation, rather than batteries of tests. I have found the writings of Malcolm Parlett, Bob Stake, Barry McDonald and Helen Simons the most helpful in the theory of evaluation, and Lawrence Stenhouse and John Elliott in relating the theory to practice.

Where should I start?

● Start with an interest or a problem that you have in your practical class-room work, or perhaps more widely in school.
● Collect information about this. Analyse the problem. Describe your interest. Clarify and focus what you want to evaluate. Collect reliable and valid information.
● Explain the facts of the situation. Think of possible explanations. Do the facts support your hypothesis?
● Brainstorm possible ways of solving the problem, or improving the situation.
● Test out the best solutions. Monitor any changes. Note improvements.
● Has anybody else an interest in this? Discuss it. Read about it. Ring up an old college tutor or your local inspector or university department of education.

We have used these action-research steps in my school in all sorts of

subjects and topics of interest, and with various problems:
  A. Review
  B. Diagnosis
  C. Planning
  D. Implementation
  E. Monitoring Effects
These processes can be used either individually or as a group.

Much more could be said about evaluation, but I hope I have covered enough to stimulate further thought and reading. We certainly need to be alert, constantly assessing, reviewing and appraising what we do, and what we expect our pupils to learn. Personal, Social and Moral Education must meet the current needs of our pupils. To do this, healthy curriculum renewal is needed. Teachers who have a sharpened awareness of assessment and evaluation techniques and skills will be the more ready to meet the challenge.

Footnotes

1. D. Slatterly, *Assessment in Schools*
2. *Personal and Social Development*.
3. Available from the Department of Education and Science, Room 2/11, Elizabeth House, York Road, London SE1 7PH.
4. J. Balogh, *Improving the Examination System*, Schools Council Programme 5.
5. See C. Power, 'A manual for coding and scoring a community meeting', unpublished doctoral thesis.
6. See E. Wasserman, A. Garold, 'Applications of Kohlberg's theory to curricula and democratic schools', Educational Analysis Vol. 5, No. 1, *Personal, Social and Moral Education*.
7. R. McCormick (ed.), *Calling Education to Account*.
8. C. Hook, *Studying Classrooms*.
9. John Elliott, 'Rationale and Procedures', *Classroom Action Research Bulletin*, No. 1.
10. John Elliott, 'Developing Hypotheses about Classrooms from Teachers' Practical Constructs', *Interchange*.
11. Readers interested in these evaluation processes would benefit by reading Colin Hook's book mentioned earlier; John Elliott's *Action-Research: a Framework for Self-Evaluation in Schools*, available from the Cambridge Institute of Education; and Clem Adleman's *Uttering, Muttering*.

PART 3

TOOLS FOR
THE JOB

REFERENCES

CHAPTER 1

G. M. Trevelyan, *Illustrated English Social History*, Pelican/Penguin Books Ltd, 1964.

M. G. Jones, *The Charity School Movement, A Study of Eighteenth Century Puritanism in Action*, quoted in G.M. Trevelyan (see above).

Religious Education in Secondary Schools, Schools Council Working Paper 36, Evans Brothers Ltd/Methuen Educational Ltd, London, 1971.

P. McPhail, H. Chapman, J. R. Ungoed-Thomas, *Lifeline*, Schools Council Moral Education Project, Longman Group Ltd, London, 1972.

Lawrence Stenhouse, *Authority, Education and Emancipation*, Consultative Committee Working Paper No. 2, Heinemann Educational Books Ltd, London, 1983.

D. H. Hamblin, *The Teacher and Counselling*, Basil Blackwell Publisher Ltd, Oxford, 1974.

K. David, *Pastoral Work and Education in Personal Relationships in Lancashire Secondary Schools*, Lancashire LEA, 1974.

Who Cares? Reading LEA, 1974.

M. Marland, *Pastoral Care*, Heinemann Educational Books Ltd, London, 1974.

D. H. Hamblin, *The Teacher and Pastoral Care*, Basil Blackwell Publisher Ltd, Oxford, 1978.

J. Baldwin, H. Wells, *Active Tutorial Work*, Basil Blackwell Publisher Ltd, Oxford, 1980.

P. McPhail, H. Chapman, J.R. Ungoed-Thomas, *Moral Education in the Secondary School*, Longman Group Ltd, London, 1972.

C. Ball, M. Ball, *Education for a Change*, Penguin Books Ltd, 1973.

Cross'd with Adversity, Schools Council Working Paper 27, Evans Brothers Ltd/Methuen Educational Ltd, London, 1970.

Careers Education in the 1970s, Schools Council Working Paper 40, Evans Brothers Ltd/Methuen Educational Ltd, London, 1972.

Social Education: an experiment in four secondary schools, Schools Council Working Paper 51, Evans Brothers Ltd/Methuen Educational Ltd, London, 1974.

B. E. Wakeman, *Social Education at Rotheram High School*, Cambridge Institute of Education, 1980.

Work, Schools Council Project, Longman Group Ltd, London, 1977–80.

M. S. Rogers, *Living Well*, Health Education Project, Cambridge University Press, 1977.

Think Well, Schools Council Health Education Project 5–13, Thomas Nelson and Sons Ltd, London, 1977.

Schools Council Health Education Project 13–18, Forbes Publications Ltd, London, 1982.

K. David, *Personal and Social Education in Secondary Schools*, Schools Council Programme 3, Longman Group Ltd, London, 1982.

Aspects of Secondary Education in England, HMSO, London, 1979.

Curriculum 11–16, HMSO, London, 1977.

Framework for the School Curriculum, HMSO, London, 1980.

Half Our Future, HMSO, London, 1963.

A View of the Curriculum, HMSO, London, 1980.

CHAPTER 2

D. Hargreaves, *The Challenge for the Comprehensive School*, Routledge and Kegan Paul Ltd, London, 1982.

Personal and Social Development, Assessment of Performance Unit, Department of Education and Science, London, 1981.

R. Pring, *Personal and Social Development*, Cambridge Journal of Education, Vol. 12, No. 1, 1982.

P. McPhail et al, *Moral Education in the Secondary School*, Longman Group Ltd, London, 1972.

P. Hirst, 'Liberal Education and the Nature of Knowledge', in *Knowledge and the Curriculum*, Routledge and Kegan Paul Ltd, London, 1974.

P. Phenix, *Realms of Meaning*, McGraw-Hill, New York, 1964.

R. Pring, *Knowledge and Schooling*, Open Books Publishing Ltd, 1976.

P. Woods, M. Hammersley (eds.), 'Having a Laugh' in *The Process of Schooling*, Routledge and Kegan Paul Ltd, London, 1976.

P. McPhail, *Social and Moral Education*, Basil Blackwell Publisher Ltd, Oxford, 1982.

Health Education, Discussion Paper No. 8, Bedfordshire Education Service, 1980.

B. Bernstein, *Class, Codes and Control*, Routledge and Kegan Paul Ltd, 1971.

CHAPTER 3

R. S. Peters, *Ethics and Education*, George Allen and Unwin (Publishers) Ltd, 1966.

D. Bridges, P. Scrimshaw, *Values and Authority in Schools*, Hodder and Stoughton Ltd, London, 1975.

S. Simon, *Meeting Yourself Halfway*, Argus Communications, Illinois, 1974.

L. Raths, M. Harmin, S. Simon, *Values and Teaching*, Charles Merrill Publishers, Columbus, 1978.

L. Kohlberg, 'Moral Stages and Moralization: The cognitive-developmental approach' in Thomas Lickona's *Moral Development and Behavior: Theory, Research and Social Issues*, Holt, Rinehart and Winston, New York, 1976.

R. H. Hersh, D. P. Paolitto, J. Reimer, *Promoting Moral Growth*, Longman Inc., New York, 1979.

J. Wilson, *A Teacher's Guide to Moral Education*, Geoffrey Chapman Publishers, 1973.

J. Wilson, 'First Steps in Moral Education' in L.O. Ward's *The Ethical Dimensions of the School Curriculum*, University College of Swansea Faculty of Education, 1982.

Wilson, *Practical Methods of Moral Education*, Heinemann Educational Books Ltd, London, 1972.

McPhail et al, *Moral Education in the Secondary School*, Longman Group Ltd, London, 1972.

Ingram, Startline Series: *Setting the Scene*, Longman Group Ltd, London, 1978.

McPhail, C. Rainbow, M. Rogers, *Living Well Programme*, Cambridge University Press, 1977.

Straughan, *Can We Teach Children to be Good?* George Allen and Unwin (Publishers) Ltd, London, 1982.

Kathleen Gow, *Yes, Virginia, There is Right and Wrong*, Wiley, 1980.

CHAPTER 4

Baldwin, H. Wells, *Active Tutorial Work*, Basil Blackwell Publisher Ltd, Oxford, 1980.

Schools Council Health Education Project 13–18, Forbes Publication Ltd, London, 1982.

Pring, *Personal and Social Development*, Cambridge Journal of Education, Vol. 12, No. 1, 1982.

Brown, *Philosophy and the Christian Faith*, Inter-Varsity Press, Leicester, 1969.

Schaeffer, *The God Who Is There*, Hodder and Stoughton Ltd, London, 1968.

Schaeffer, *Escape from Reason*, Inter-Varsity Press, Leicester, 1968.

Schaeffer, *Death in the City*, Inter-Varsity Press, Leicester, 1969.

Chapman, *The Case for Christianity*, Lion Publishing plc, Hertfordshire, 1972.

Matthew, *It's all in the mind—or is The Strong Hold of Intellectualism*, Restoration, Bradford, 1983.

CHAPTER 5

Lawrence Stenhouse, *An Introduction Curriculum Research and Development*, Heinemann Educational Books Ltd, London, 1975.

Tyler, *Basic Principles of Curriculum and Instruction*, University of Chicago Press, 1949.

Kenneth David, *Personal and Social Education in Secondary Schools*, Longman Group Ltd, London, 1982.

B. Crick, A. Porter (eds.), *Political Education and Political Literacy*, Longman Group Ltd, London, 1978.

L. Button, *Group Tutoring for the Form Tutor*, Hodder and Stoughton Ltd, London, 1982.

CHAPTER 6

K. David, *Pastoral Work and Education in Personal Relationship in Lancashire Secondary Schools*, Lancashire LEA, 1974.

Health Education, Discussion Paper No. 8, Bedfordshire Education Service, 1980.

B. Crick, A. Porter (eds.), *Political Education and Political Literacy*, Longman Group Ltd, London, 1978.

CHAPTER 7

K. David, *Personal and Social Education in Secondary Schools*, Longman Group Ltd, London, 1982.

CHAPTER 8

L. Button, *Group Tutoring for the Form Tutor*, Hodder and Stoughton Ltd, London, 1982.

P. McPhail, *Social and Moral Education*, Basil Blackwell Publisher Ltd, Oxford, 1982

P. McPhail, H. Chapman, J. R. Ungoed-Thomas, *Lifeline*, Schools Council Moral Education Project, Longman Group Ltd, London, 1972.

S. Thompson, J. H. Kahn, *The Group Process as a Helping Technique*, Pergamon Press Ltd, Oxford, 1970.

Lawrence Stenhouse, 'Controversial Values Issues in the Classroom' in W. G. Carr's *Values and the Curriculum*, National Education Association, Washington, 1970.

P. McPhail, *Social and Moral Education*, Basil Blackwell Publisher Ltd, Oxford, 1982.

J. Baldwin, H. Wells, *Active Tutorial Work*, Basil Blackwell Publisher Ltd, Oxford, 1980.

Think Well, Schools Council Health Education Project, Thomas Nelson and Sons Ltd, London, 1977.

Living Well, Health Education Council Project, Cambridge University Press, 1977.

Work: Part 2, Schools Council Careers Education and Guidance Project, Longman Group Ltd, London, 1978.

S. Simon, *Meeting Yourself Halfway*, Argus Communications, Illinois, 1974.

P. Phillips, F. Cordell, *Am I OK?* Argus Communications, Illinois, 1975.

D. Brandes, H. Phillips, *Gamesters' Handbook*, Hutchinson Publishing Group Ltd, London, 1977.

H. Lewis, H. Streitfeld, *Growth Games*, Abacus Press/Sphere Books Ltd, London, 1973.

D. H. Hamblin, *The Teacher and Counselling*, Basil Blackwell Publisher Ltd, Oxford, 1974.

D. H. Hamblin, *The Teacher and Pastoral Care*, Basil Blackwell Publisher Ltd, Oxford, 1978.

D. H. Hamblin, *Teaching Study Skills*, Basil Blackwell Publisher Ltd, Oxford, 1981.

Lawrence Stenhouse, *Humanities Curriculum Project*, Heinemann Educational Books Ltd, London, 1970.

The Childwall Project: *The Responsibilities of Adulthood, Understanding Children, Living Today, The World Around Us*, E. J. Arnold and Son Ltd, Leeds, 1972–74.

Social Education Kits: Marriage and Homemaking, Conservation, Consumer Education, Towards Tomorrow, The British, MacMillan Education Ltd, London, 1976.

J. Ashdown, *Interpersonal-Behaviour, Training Games, Techniques and Procedures*, Berkshire Training Agency, 1972.

B. E. Wakeman, *Mixed Ability Teaching: Problems and Possibilities, Using Nominal Group Technique*, Schools Council TIQL Project, Cambridge Institute of Education, 1982.

B. S. Collinson, S. F. Dunlap, *School Counsellor*, Vol. 26, No. 1, 1978.

CHAPTER 9

D. Slatterly, *Assessment in Schools*, Basil Blackwell Publisher Ltd, Oxford, 1981.

Personal and Social Development, Assessment and Performance Unit, Department of Education and Science, London, 1981.

J. Balogh, 'Profile Reports for School Leavers', in *Improving the Examination*

BOOKS, TEACHING MATERIALS AND AIDS

System, Schools Council Programme 5, Longman Group Ltd, London, 1982.

Vocational Preparation, City and Guilds Course 365, City and Guilds, London.

Keeping the School Under Review, ILEA, 1977.

R. McCormick, *Calling Education to Account*, Heinemann Educational Books Ltd, London, 1982.

C. Hook, *Studying Classrooms*, Deakin University, Victoria, 1981.

J. Elliott, *The Ford Teaching Project*, Cambridge Institute of Education, 1977.

J. Elliott, 'Rationale and Procedures', Classroom Action Research Bulletin No. 1, Cambridge Institute of Education, 1977.

J. Elliott, *Teacher-Pupil Interaction and the Quality of Learning Project*, Schools Council TIQL Project, Cambridge Institute of Education, 1984.

J. Elliott, 'Developing Hypotheses about Classrooms from Teachers' Practical Constructs', *Interchange* Vol. 7, No. 2, 1976–77.

J. Elliott, *Action-Research: A Framework for Self-Evaluation in Schools*, Cambridge Institute of Education, 1981.

C. Adleman, *Uttering, Muttering*, Grant McIntyre Ltd, London, 1981.

C. Power, *A Manual for Coding and Scoring a Community Meeting*, University of Boston, 1977.

E. Wasserman, A. Garold, Applications of Kolberg's theory to curricula and democratic schools, Educational Analysis, Vol. 5, No. 1, *Personal, Social and Moral Education*, Falmer Press, Lewis, 1983.

This is an amended list of those displayed at the DES course 'Ethics and the Curriculum' at Reading University, 1983.

MORE ABOUT THEORY

Authority, Education and Emancipation, Lawrence Stenhouse, Heinemann Educational Books Ltd, 1983. A collection of papers by a leading thinker in values, education and curriculum development.

Authority, Responsibility and Education, R. S. Peters, George Allen and Unwin (Publishers) Ltd, 1973. Some clear thinking by a well-known educationalist.

Beyond the Numbers Game, D. Hamilton, D. Jenkins, C. King, B. MacDonald, M. Parlett (eds.), MacMillan Education Ltd, 1977.

Calling Education to Account, R. McCormick (ed.), Heinemann Educational Books Ltd, 1982. Open University set book on evaluation.

Can We Teach Children To Be Good? R. Straughan, George Allen and Unwin (Publishers) Ltd, 1982. A helpful introduction for teachers.

A Century of Moral Philosophy, W. D. Hudson, Lutterworth Press, 1980. A very useful introduction to Moral Philosophy.

The Ethical Dimensions of the School Curriculum, L. Ward (ed.), University of Swansea Faculty of Education, 1982. A symposium of articles by leading writers in PSME.

The Group Process as a Helping Technique, S. Thompson, J. H. Kahn, Pergamon Press Ltd, 1970. A textbook on group work.

Historical Selections in the Philosophy of Religion, N. Smart, SCM Press, 1962. A useful reference volume on my bookshelves.

A History of Sociological Analysis, T. Bottomore, R. Nisbet (eds.), Heinemann Educational Books Ltd, 1978. A collection of articles on key themes of modern sociology.

Ideas: A Guide to Moral and Metaphysical Outlooks, J. Wilson, Lutterworth Press, 1972. A slim volume for handy and quick reference.

An Introduction to Curriculum Research and Development, Lawrence Stenhouse, Heinemann Educational Books Ltd, 1975. The Open University textbook on curriculum studies.

Knowledge and the Curriculum, P. H. Hirst, Routledge and Kegan Paul Ltd, 1974. A collection of philosophical papers.

The Limits and Possibilities of Schooling, C. Hearne, Allyn and Bacon Inc., 1978. An introduction to the sociology of education.

Patterns of Community Education, E. Midwinter, Ward Lock Educational Co. Ltd, 1973. Stimulating reading about the relating of education to the community's social situation.

Personal, Social and Moral Education, R. Pring (ed.), Falmer Press, 1983. A collection of articles about this field in the Educational Analysis Series, Vol. 5 No. 1. A must for interested readers. Particularly good about Kohlberg. An extensive bibliography.

The Process of Schooling, M. Hammersley, P. Woods (eds.), Routledge and Kegan Paul Ltd, 1976. An Open University reader.

The Psychology of Learning, R. Berger, A. E. M. Seaborne, Pelican/Penguin Books Ltd, 1976. A discussion of laws, theories and models of learning.

The Psychology of Thinking, R. Thomson, Pelican/Penguin Books Ltd, 1959.

The Sociology of Education, O. Banks

tsford (B.T.) Ltd, 1968. An older xtbook for generations of students in acher-training.

wards Moral and Religious Maturity, Brusselmans, Silver Burdett Co, 80. A heavyweight volume on the st International Conference on Moral d Religious Development.

e Unshakable Kingdom and the changing Person, E. S. Jones, ingdon Press, 1972. An explanation the concept and principles of the gdom of God: inspiring reading.

ORE ABOUT RELATING HEORY TO PRACTICE

tive Tutorial Work, J. Baldwin, Wells, Basil Blackwell Publisher Ltd, 79. This is a mine of ideas, activities, mes, strategies and teaching hniques for pastoral work. Essential rchase.

e Bull Ring, A. J. Grainger, rgamon Press Ltd, 1970. A class- om experiment in Moral Education.

e Challenge for the Comprehensive, H. Hargreaves, Routledge and gan Paul Ltd, 1982. Culture, rriculum and Community — a much cussed and quoted book.

anging Schools, Changing rriculum, M. Galton, B. Moon s.), Harper and Row Ltd, 1983. A de-ranging symposium of papers m the Association for the Study of Curriculum, Easter Conference 32. The paper by J. Elliott is ticularly rich.

ildren's Wellbeing, J. Brierley, ER-Nelson Publishing Co. Ltd, 1980. owth, development and learning m conception to adolescence.

mbatting Racialism in Schools, tional Union of Teachers, 1981.

mmunication and Social Skills, Lorac, M. Weiss, Pergamon Press /A. Wheaton and Co., 1981. A hools Council Communication and cial Skills Project.

mmunity Service, Social Education the Curriculum, P. Scrimshaw, dder and Stoughton Ltd, 1981. Very eresting to teachers involved in mmunity service.

Bono's Thinking Course, E. de no, BBC Publications, 1982. hough controversial in educational les there are several strategies here great value in PSME as well as in teaching of thinking.

Decision-making for Schools and Colleges, Dean F. Juniper, Pergamon Press Ltd, 1976. A number of techniques and ideas for teachers.

Drama and the Whole Curriculum, J. Nixon (ed.), Hutchinson Educational Ltd, 1982. A survey of the vital contribution of drama to the curriculum.

Economic and Industrial Awareness in the School Curriculum, Bedfordshire Education Service, 1983. A consideration of how best to include studies aimed at enhancing pupils' understanding of industrial Britain and the economy.

Education for Responsibility, Bedfordshire Education Service, 1981. Discussion Paper No. 10. Well worth reading.

Field Research, L. Schatzman, A. L. Strauss, Prentice-Hall International Inc., 1973. A practical volume on how to go about field research. Highly recommended.

Gamesters' Handbook, D. Brandes, H. Phillips, Hutchinson Educational Ltd, 1979. One hundred-and-four games for teachers and group leaders. Full of ideas.

A Groundplan for the Study of Religion, Schools Council Religious Education Committee, Schools Council, 1977. A very useful pamphlet on curriculum planning.

Group Tutoring for the Form Teacher, L. Button, Hodder and Stoughton Ltd, 1982. Here is a clear and sequential programme of help for teachers to make positive use of pastoral time. Every secondary school staff-room should have a copy.

Growth Games, H. R. Lewis, H. S. Streitfeld, Abacus Books Ltd/Sphere Books Ltd, 1973. Two hundred ways of developing human potential. Much can be learned from this book. Needs discernment.

Hard Times Catalog for Youth Ministry, M. Benson, D. Benson, Group Books, 1982.

Health Education, Bedfordshire Education Service, 1980. Discussion Paper No. 8. A very useful paper.

Health Education 13–18, Forbes Publications Ltd, 1982. A Schools Council Health Education Project. This is a package of a teacher-guide and curriculum materials based on a work-sheet approach which is essential to schools with Health Education

programmes. The Co-ordinator's guide is excellent. The Project team provide in-service courses and back-up for teachers. One of the most useful projects to be published.

Health Education in the Secondary School, Schools Council Working Paper No. 57, Evans Brothers Ltd/ Methuen Educational Ltd, 1976. There is still a lot of help here.

Human Relationships for Schools and Colleges, Dean F. Juniper, Cressrelles Publishing Co. Ltd, 1977. Lots of useful material here to bring insights and procedures of counselling into the curriculum.

In Black and White, National Union of Teachers, 1979. Guidelines for teachers on racial stereotyping in textbooks and learning materials.

In Other People's Shoes, P. McPhail, Longman Group Ltd/Schools Council, 1972. A Schools Council Project in Moral Education. This is an introduction to the materials: Sensitivity, Consequences and Points of View. There is much practical help for the class-room here. These class-room materials need resurrecting from those dusty cupboards, and using by imaginative teachers: it is unfortunate that the publishers have no plans to reprint.

Journeys into Religion, Hart-Davis Educational Ltd, 1977. A Schools Council Religious Education in Secondary Schools Project. Teacher's Handbook.

Meeting Yourself Halfway, S. Simon, Argus Communications, 1974. The principles of Values Clarification techniques and thirty-one strategies, many of which can be used in the class-room.

Moral Development: A Guide to Piaget and Kohlberg, R. Duska and M. Whelan, Gill and Macmillan Ltd, 1977. A guide to Piaget and Kohlberg with a Roman Catholic perspective.

Moral Education in the Secondary School, P. McPhail, J. R. Ungoed-Thomas, H. Chapman, Longman Group Ltd/Schools Council, 1972. Still one of the most important books on the subject.

Parents Listen, Girls Talk, Boys Talk, L. Pickering, Fowler Wright Books Ltd/Geoffrey Chapman Publishers, 1981. A series which provides a source of ideas for teachers.

Pastoral Work and Education in Personal Relationships in Lancashire Secondary Schools, K. David, Lancashire LEA, 1974. A helpful survey of publications, teaching materials and sources of information.

Personal and Social Development, Department of Education and Science, 1981. The Assessment of Performance Unit. Essential reading, particularly on mapping PSME.

Personal and Social Education in Secondary Schools, K. David, Longman Group Ltd/Schools Council, 1982. Schools Council Programme 3. Essential reading on the whole area.

Political Education and Political Literacy, B. Crick, A. Porter (eds.), Longman Group Ltd, 1978. Report and papers of working party of Hansard Society. A source-book for every teacher interested in politics.

Problems and Practice of Pastoral Care, D. H. Hamblin (ed.), Basil Blackwell Publisher Ltd, 1981. A must for any teacher interested in pastoral care.

Promoting Moral Growth from Piaget to Kohlberg, R. Hersh, D. P. Paolitto, J. Reimer, Longman Inc., 1979. An excellent guide, clearly written and interesting to read.

Real Questions, David Field, Peter Toon, Lion Publishing plc, 1982. Key questions about behaviour and faith: issues clarified and routes to possible answers given from an evangelical Christian viewpoint.

Religious Education in Secondary Schools, Evans Brothers Ltd/Methuen Educational Ltd, 1971. Schools Council Working Paper 36. Still provides a useful summary of the curriculum development in RE.

School Accountability, J. Elliott, D. Bridges, D. Ebbutt, R. Gibson, J. Nias, Grant McIntyre Ltd, 1981. An account of the SSRC Accountability Project in Cambridge.

Social Education: An Experiment in Four Secondary Schools, J. Rennie, E. A. Lunzer, W. T. Williams, Evans Brothers Ltd/Methuen Educational Ltd, 1974. Schools Council Working Paper 51. Interesting to read and ask, 'How far have we really come since the 1970s?'

Social Education and Social Understanding, J. Elliott, R. Pring, University of London Press Ltd, 1975. I recommend these authors who are always stimulating reading.

Social and Moral Education, P. McPhail, Basil Blackwell Publisher Ltd, 1982. An interesting summary of McPhail's current thinking.

The Teacher and Counselling, D. H. Hamblin, Basil Blackwell Publisher Ltd, 1974. An invaluable book on pastoral care.

The Teacher and Pastoral Care, D. H. Hamblin, Basil Blackwell Publisher Ltd, 1978. I recommend every secondary school to buy this and the other three books by the same author.

A Teachers' Guide to Action Research, Jon Nixon (ed.), Grant McIntyre Ltd, 1981. Examples of teachers' work in action research.

Teaching Study Skills, D.H. Hamblin, Basil Blackwell Publisher Ltd, 1981. Highly recommended.

The Tutor, K. Blackburn, Heinemann Educational Books Ltd, 1975. A seminal thinker about pastoral care and tutorial work.

TEACHING MATERIALS IN THE CLASS-ROOM

Am I OK? P. L. Phillip, F. D. Cordell, Argus Communications, 1975. A practical guide to transactional analysis, and to genuine personal growth.

Awareness Through Drama, T. O'Regan, Edupak, 1982. A collection of playlets on teenage situations which provide starters for discussion and exploration of relationship themes. It also inspires teachers to write their own dialogues about issues current in school life.

Breakaway Series: *People with Problems*, *Where the Money Goes*, P. A. Sauvain, Hulton Educational Publications Ltd.

Checkpoints: *Advertising*, V. Thom, *Alcohol and Tobacco*, J. L. Foster, *Drug Takers*, J. L. Foster, *From 0–5*, *The Pre-School Years*, J. L. Foster, *Growing Old*, F. Leigh, *The Police*, J. L. Foster, *Prejudice*, V. Thom, *Prisons*, J. L. Foster, *Television*, R. Robinson, *Trades Unions*, F. Leigh *Unmarried Mothers*, J. L. Foster, Edward Arnold (Publishers) Ltd, 1974–80. Newspaper type of format. These are popular with young people and provide helpful starting-points fo the teacher.

The Childwall Project: *Living Today*, *The Responsibilities of Adulthood*, *Understanding Children*, *The World Around Us*, E. J. Arnold and Son Ltd 1972–74. Multi-media curriculum packages. Excellent material which ca still be used.

Claims, Benefits and Rights, G. Dauncey, CRAC, 1983. Excellent f Careers Guidance teachers.

The Counterpoint Series: *Crime and Justice*, *Family and Friends*, *Medicine and Morality*, *Prejudice and Discrimination*, P. Moss, George G. Harrap and Co. Ltd, 1974–78. A very useful series but rather wordy for less able pupils.

Death, M. Ball, Oxford University Press, 1976. Needs sensitive handling but provides a learning resource on a almost taboo subject.

Earning a Living, K. Allsop, M. Leipe Ginn & Co. Ltd, 1971. Choosing and finding a job.

Enquiries Series: *Aggression*, *Communication*, *Courtship*, *Drugs*, *Family Life*, *Learning*, W. J. Hanson, Longman Group Ltd, 1973–77. This i an excellent series of class-room books, which teachers like and pupils enjoy.

Facing Unemployment, G. Dauncey, CRAC, 1983. An excellent workbook for Careers Education.

Harrap New Generation Series: *The Law*, T. Forbes, P. Sommer, George G. Harrap and Co. Ltd, 1972.

Human Society, C. Hambling, P. Matthews, MacMillan Education Ltd, 1975. A very useful book for CSE and O Level Sociology students.

Humanism, B. Smoker, Ward Lock Educational Co. Ltd, 1973. An introduction to Humanism in the Living Religions Series.

In-Focus Series: *The Communicators*, I. Learmonth, *Crime and Punishment*, D. Church, B. Ford, *The Developing Nations*, N. Dalgleigh, *Focus on Health*, A. Birkett, *The Law in Action*, M.W. Thomas, *Looking After Yourself*, I. Lockett, *Looking at Marriage*, G. West, J. Loeb, Y. Beecham, *Managing Your Money*, M. W. Thomas, *People in Need*, M. W. Thomas, *Someone to turn to*, D. Arthur, *Something to do*, H. Dobinson, *Somewhere to Live*, D. Church, B. Ford, Thomas Nelson and Sons Ltd, 1970–75. These books are still useful, although they are dating, as topical subjects do so quickly.

Insight into Society: *Danger*, C. Clutterbuck, *Family Life*, J. Taylor, *Last Days*, J. Martin, E.J. Arnold and Son Ltd, 1978.

It's Your Choice, M. Lynch, Edward Arnold (Publishers) Ltd, 1977. A series of role play and simulation exercises on environmental and social themes. They teach social and communication skills and are very successful with 15 to 16-year-olds.

It's Your Life, A Personal and Social Course, M. Cheston, A. Wheaton and Co., 1979. Here is a useful text book for class use on 'Yourself', 'Your Surroundings', and 'Your relationships'. Busy teachers will find this a great help, and it is attractive to the 14–16 age range.

Living Well: *How are we feeling today?* P. McPhail, *Support Group*, C. Rainbow, Cambridge University Press, 1977. Work cards that are valuable materials for imaginative and skilled teachers. An excellent teacher's guide on various relationship, choice and health issues for young people.

Love and Marriage, M. Samuda,

Pergamon Press Ltd/A. Wheaton and Co., 1976. An anthology.

My Job Application File, G. Dauncey, CRAC, 1983. Invaluable aid for those involved in Careers Guidance in schools.

Natural Nashers, University of Cambridge, 1982. A Health Education Council and Dental Health Study Project. A kit for class-room use.

New Horizons: Opinions and Attitudes, S. Joyce, William Collins, Sons and Co. Ltd, 1980. A very helpful book, especially for teachers new to PSME.

Pic Points, P. Weir, V. Weir, Redemptorist Publications, 1982. We have used this book extensively with class groups.

Problem Page, S. Porter, Edward Arnold (Publishers) Ltd, 1979. A useful classbook which also provides inspiration for teachers to write their own material.

Responsible Living: *It's up to you*, *Working with Other People*, C. G. Martin, Hulton Educational Publications Ltd, 1973–74.

Rights, Responsibilities and the Law, J. Edmunds, Thomas Nelson and Sons Ltd, 1982. A practical guide and workbook for 14–19s on the law and rights and responsibilities. Produced jointly with ILEA learning materials service.

School, J. L. Foster, Pergamon Press Ltd/A. Wheaton and Co. Ltd. An anthology.

The Schools Council/Nuffield Humanities Project. For Humanities Curriculum Project see Working Paper 56, *Dissemination of Innovation*, Evans Brothers Ltd/Methuen and Co. Ltd, 1976. Multi-media packs of class-room resources on controversial human themes: relations between the sexes, people and work, race . . . See *Humanities Curriculum Project*, Lawrence Stenhouse, Heinemann Educational Books Ltd, 1970. The epoch-making work of Stenhouse and his associates in HCP appears to be misunderstood or overlooked in some PSME circles. The debate about 'procedural neutrality', and an understanding of the HCP class-room methodology is still key to working out our stance on values education. The packs of resources are invaluable evidence for discussion even if you reject the HCP philosophy.

Serendipity, Youth Bible Study Series: *Belonging, Directions, Front Line,*

Hassles, Knowing Me, Starters, Torn Between, The Way Ahead, X-certificate, L. Coleman, D. Rydberg, Scripture Union, 1983. An excellent series of student books for 11–19s in Christian education, and leaders' manuals. Refreshing and lively, on a variety of identity, moral, relationship and belief issues. Bible-centred. Highly recommended for ideas in the class-room.

Social Education: *The British, Conservation, Consumer Education, Freedom and Responsibility, Marriage and Homemaking, Towards Tomorrow*, The North West Regional Curriculum Development Project, MacMillan Education Ltd, 1976. I relied heavily on these packages of worksheets in the 1970s. They can still be used, where not dated.

Social Studies, An Introduction, J. Nobbs, MacMillan Education Ltd, 1979.

Sociology, J. Nobbs, B. Hine, M. Flemming, MacMillan Education Ltd, 1979.

Themes for Living: Right and Wrong, G. Parrinder, Hulton Educational Publications Ltd, 1973.

Think Strips: *It'll Never Be the Same, It's My Life, It's Not Easy, It's Only Fair, It's Your Round, Loosers Weepers, Seeing's Believing*, Longman Group Ltd, 1981. A very popular series with 15 to 16-year-olds about social, moral and personal issues.

What Are We Going to Do? B. Ridgeway, Edward Arnold (Publishers) Ltd, 1982. A useful classbook for Careers work.

Who Cares? 'Living Well', M. S. Rogers, Cambridge University Press, 1977. Health Education Council Project 13–18. A collection of some forty dialogues about human relationships which can be used in group work as 'case studies' for role play and discussion. An invaluable source.

Your First Move, P. March, T. Western, Hobsons Press Ltd, 1982. Part of the Survival and Job Skills Series.

AUDIO VISUAL AIDS

CMAC Centre tapes: *Coping with Conscience*, *Coping with the Opposite Sex*, *Coping with People*, CMAC. School Discussion Starters.

Current television and radio programmes. Consult the schedules of the relevant broadcasting companies. We use the following: BBC Education, Radio and Television 'Child Care', 15–16, 'Exploring Society', 13–15, 'Going to Work', 14–16, 'In the News', 9–12, 'In Your Own Time', 15–19, 'Lifetime', 15+, 'Social Studies: Teenage Plays', 'Scene', 14–16; ITV 'Facts for Life', 15–18, 'Good Health', 8–12, 'Living and Growing', 10–13, 'Making a Living', 14+, 'Parenthood', 14+.

Disease and Health, E. Ortleb, R. Codice, Millikcn Publications, 1969. Overhead projector transparency set.

Foods and Your Health, E. Ortleb, R. Codice, Milliken Publications, 1969. Overhead projector transparency set.

'How the Nations are Governed', Newsweek Multimedia Programme, 1977. Audio-visual stimulus materials.

Immigration, N. Fromer, Mary Glasgow Publications, 1979. Audio-visual stimulus materials.

Martin Luther King, Mary Glasgow Publications. Audio-visual stimulus materials.

The Police, B. Fromer, Mary Glasgow Publications, 1981. Audio-visual presentation.

Prejudice, B. Kennedy, Mary Glasgow Publications, 1979.

Rites of Passage: *Birth*, *Initiation*, *Marriage* and *Death*, Mary Glasgow Publications, 1980. Audio-visual production: excellent material.

We have made extensive use of 16mm films hired from various sources, and borrowed from our local Health Education Centre. Films date fairly quickly, however, and we are making much more use of video recording which is more flexible. Schools can wipe off programmes no longer required, have a wider range of programmes, and once the heavy capital outlay is expended, it becomes a less expensive medium.